Martoni's
Pilgrimage
1394

to the centre of the
world and back

Translated from the Latin by

John Mole

First published by Fortune in 2017

www.fortunebooks.org

This translation copyright © John Mole

ISBN:978-0-9557569-8-6

Printed and bound by CPI Group (UK) Ltd, Croydon, CR0 4YY

Cover illustration: Sinai and
St Catherine's Monastery
by pilgrim Jacopo da Verona, 1335.

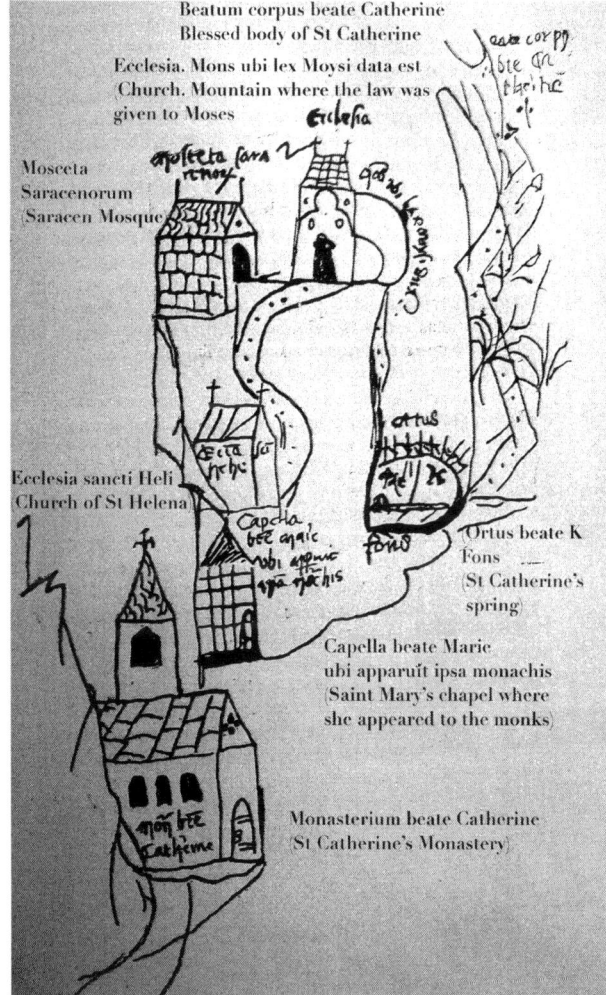

Beatum corpus beate Catherine
Blessed body of St Catherine

Ecclesia. Mons ubi lex Moysi data est
Church. Mountain where the law was
given to Moses

Mosceta
Saracenorum
(Saracen Mosque)

Ecclesia sancti Heli
(Church of St Helena)

Ortus beate K
Fons
(St Catherine's
spring)

Capella beate Marie
ubi apparuit ipsa monachis
(Saint Mary's chapel where
she appeared to the monks)

Monasterium beate Catherine
(St Catherine's Monastery)

For my family and other pilgrims

CONTENTS

MAPS ii

INTRODUCTION v

THE JOURNEY

I   From Gaeta to Alexandria   1

II   Description of Egypt   11

III   The Sinai Desert   33

IV   Jerusalem   43

V   From Jerusalem to Jaffa   56

VI   From Jaffa to Cyprus   58

VII   Cyprus   61

VIII   From Cyprus to Rhodes   73

IX   The Cycladic Islands   79

X   Athens, Chalcis, Corinth   86

XI   From Corinth to Italy   99

XII   Through Italy to Carinola   107

POSTSCRIPT   111

ACKNOWLEDGEMENTS   117

THE TRANSLATOR   119

Martoni's itinerary

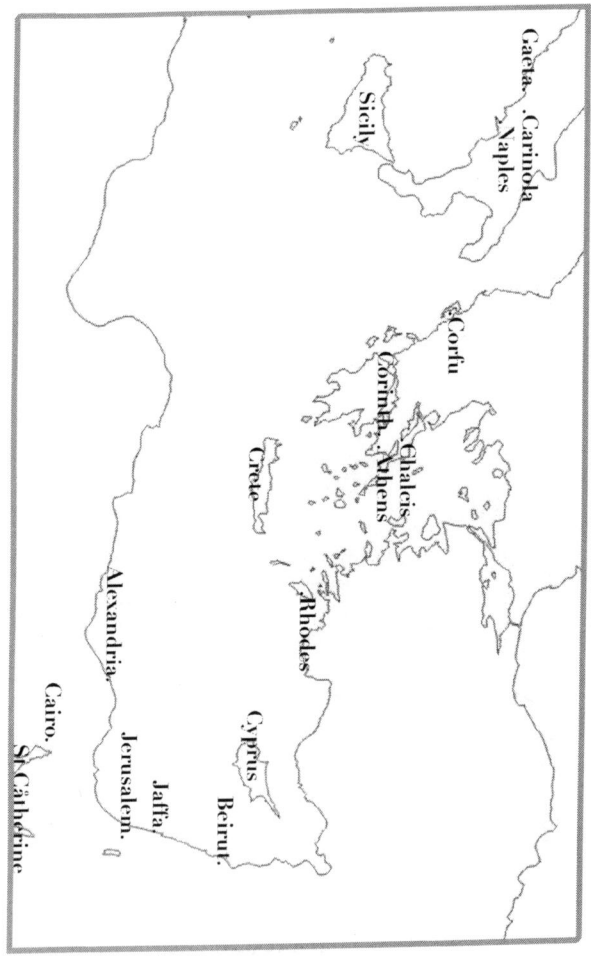

Eastern Mediterranean powers 1395

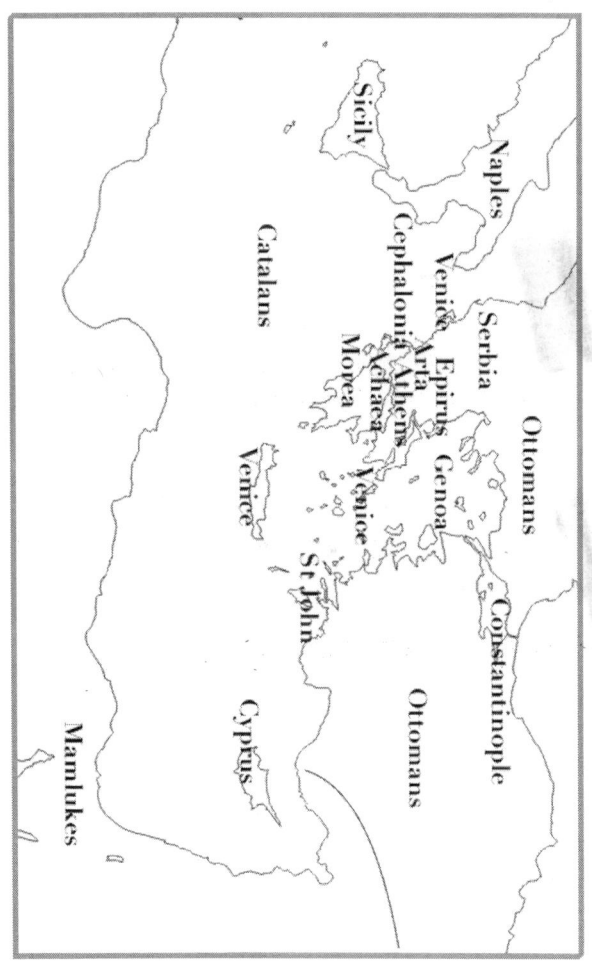

INTRODUCTION

An extraordinary journey by an ordinary man.

Nicola Martoni made a pilgrimage from Italy to Jerusalem in 1394. He was a middle-aged provincial lawyer from a small town near Naples. He travelled across the Mediterranean through the Greek islands to Egypt, across the Sinai desert to Jerusalem and back to Italy on a dangerous and adventurous journey, braving shipwreck, pirates and brigands.

He wrote about his pilgrimage at about the same time that Chaucer wrote about his. The resemblance ends there. He was not an aristocrat, a monk, a scholar, a writer, but as 'ordinary' as anyone who was literate and comfortably well-off. As far as we know, he was writing for no wider audience than himself, his family and friends. He confesses to being little and short-sighted, gullible, timid and often frightened. But he has the strength of character to overcome his weaknesses in the face of adversity and remain open, curious, eager to explore. Although his experiences might have been useful to people planning a pilgrimage, if only demonstrating what to avoid, it is not a travel guide. It is a travel journal, a personal account that is as much about the traveller as the places travelled to.

Martoni lived in a world before the Printing Revolution, the Renaissance, the Scientific Revolution, the Reformation, the Enlightenment, the Age of Discovery, the Industrial Revolution, the Digital Revolution and all the other forces that have moulded our own minds in the last six hundred years. His journal gives us a rare insight into a medieval mind.

The translation

I translated Martoni's diary because it is a great story that deserves a wider audience than Medieval scholars. Pilgrims, travellers, tourists, believers, non-believers and general readers of all kinds will find plenty to interest them. The intention was to make the text immediate and avoid archaisms, obscurity, footnotes, anything that creates a barrier to Martoni's sense. Otherwise I have followed the text as closely as possible. I have given the places their modern names so that you can follow in Martoni's footsteps, if only on a map. The names Martoni uses are in parentheses.

The text

The text was edited by Leon Le Grand and published in Revue de l'Orient Latin, Volume III, 1894. The manuscript is in the French Bibliothèque Nationale. It is a copy made in 1397 by Ciccio Grosso di Balsorano on the instruction of Roger de Celano of La Rocca Spa of Mondragone. Martoni's original text and notes do not survive.

The Latin text is included *Martoni's Pilgrimage - in English and Latin*   ISBN: 978-0-9557569-9-3

Martoni's Latin

Martoni's Latin was the workaday tool of the legal profession and the clergy. It is a language in transition from its classical roots to the vernacular of his dialect. Even making this allowance, he does not write it as well as contemporaries. At the beginning it reads like a lawyerly deposition, ponderous and formal, the solemn statement and repetition of information. As the journal unfolds and he sloughs off his lawyer's personality, his style becomes more spontaneous and intimate and personal but he still struggles to make an elegant sentence. What the text lacks in style it makes up for in an engaging immediacy.

The political landscape

The political landscape of the Aegean and its hinterland was a kaleidoscope of empires, kingdoms, dukedoms, islands, city states, robber bands and pirate gangs, trading, competing and warring with each other. They can be roughly divided into three traditions: Catholic Christians speaking Latin languages, Orthodox Christians speaking Greek, Arabic or Syriac, Muslims speaking Arabic or Turkish. Among them were important communities with other languages or religions, for example Jews, Serbs, Albanians. The following is a brief and (over)-simplified summary of the cultures Martoni encountered.

Italy

Italy was a patchwork of competing states and warring armies. Martoni's home of Carinola and Gaeta, where he sailed from, belonged to the Kingdom of Naples.

Venice

Venice was the dominant Latin power in the Adriatic and Aegean. Strategically important islands, such as Crete, Evia and Corfu were under its direct rule. Other more or less autonomous dukedoms and islands owed it their allegiance and survival. The Dukedom of the Archipelago, with its three hundred or so islands, was the most significant.

The Byzantine Empire

The Byzantine Empire was not known as such by its inhabitants. Successors to the Roman Empire, they called it Romania and themselves Romans. The name stuck to areas which were no longer under Byzantine control but were predominantly Greek-speaking. In the journal I have translated Romania as Greece.

The Byzantine Empire was irretrievably weakened by the depredations of the Fourth Crusade. In 1204 crusaders, led by Venice, captured and looted Constantinople, deposed the Emperor, and seized many of its Aegean lands to create a new Latin Empire. Constantinople was recovered by the Byzantine Palaiologue dynasty, but was under ever increasing threat from Turks, who laid siege to it in 1394. Byzantium survived with a final flourish in the Despotate of the Morea in the Peloponnese, from its capital Mistra. (Despot means simply 'Lord' with no connotations of a style of government). Although reduced in territory, Byzantium survived in the language, religions, and culture of Greek communities in almost every foreign-dominated realm.

Latin States

By Martoni's time, the crusaders' Latin Empire had long fractured into competing kingdoms and principalities. The Dukedom of Athens was held by the Duke of Florence. The Duke of Cephalonia managed to retain the independence of his island along with Zakynthos and Ithaka. The Kingdom of Cyprus, originally established by Richard the Lionheart, existed on sufferance of Genoa which was interested in holding Famagusta only for purposes of trade.

Turkey

Turkey ruled Anatolia from its capital Edirne. It was making inroads into the Aegean and in fifty years time, 1452, would send seismic shockwaves through Christendom by taking Constantinople. Shortly before Martoni's journey, they took Thessaly, the eastern half of the Greek mainland bordering on the Dukedom of Athens to the south and the Despotate of Arta to the west. The Despotate of Arta was created and ruled by Albanians in the western half of the Greek mainland, under the protection of Serbia, itself a vassal kingdom of Turkey.

Egypt

Egypt and Greater Syria, including Jerusalem and the Holy Land, were ruled by the Mamlukes, under their elected Sultan based in Cairo. Mamlukes were Turkish-speaking freed slaves from the Crimea, Circassia and other Caucasian peoples. They appointed emirs to cities and territories, the most important being the vice-regent in Cairo, with whom the pilgrims registered. Although the Mamlukes spoke Turkish among themselves, the official language and that of the population was Arabic. Egyptian Muslims were called Saracens by the Latins. Other subjects included the virtually autonomous communities of Jews and Coptic Christians.

Stateless Powers

Based on the island of Rhodes, Hospitallers or the Order of St John, formerly of Jerusalem, now of Rhodes and soon to be evicted by the Turks to Malta, was the last remnant of the Christian Kingdom of Jerusalem. The knights, who were also monks, were recruited from all over Christendom. Their mission was both military and monastic, to resist further Muslim incursion and to protect and care for pilgrims.

The Navarrese Company was military and certainly not monastic. It was a company of French mercenaries primarily from Navarre and Gascony. When Martoni came across them they ruled what remained of the Principality of Achaea, part of the old Latin Empire, on the north coast of the Peloponnese.

Catalan mercenaries, pirates and robbers were descendants of the once powerful and feared Catalan Company of mercenaries, until finally defeated and evicted from their possessions in Central Greece by the Navarrese in 1390.

India and Indians

In Cairo Martoni calls on the Patriarch of the Oriental Orthodox Church, whose patriarchate included Greater and Lesser India as well as Coptic Egypt. Since classical times India was the world east of Jerusalem and west of China. It would have included the Middle East, Arabia and Ethiopia. Martoni meets Indian pilgrims, who could have come from anywhere between Mesopotamia and Kerala. The *Oriental* Orthodox Church should not be confused with the *Eastern* Orthodox Church, often known simply as the Orthodox Church, whose Patriarch is based in Constantinople.

Indulgences

Various sites in the Holy Land bestow an indulgence on the pilgrim. An indulgence is the remittance of temporal punishment due to sin, either on this earth or in the after-life. It can only be given if the sinner has repented and been given absolution at the sacrament of confession. An indulgence may be partial or plenary. The partial indulgences described by Martoni are all of seven years. This does not mean the duration of the punishment but the remission to be obtained by performing a penance for the specified period of time. A plenary indulgence remits all punishment.

At sea

Martoni travels on various types of vessel from small boats to large cargo ships. The differences between them were in the number of masts, whether powered by oars or wind, whether steered by an oar or by a rudder, whether they were decked or open, whether they had a poop deck at the bow or a quarter deck at the stern, providing cabins. There was no standard configuration or consistent names for types of vessel. Martoni specifically refers to a pinnace and a brigantine, but other than they probably had two masts it is hard to know exactly what they were. He also mentions galleys, which were usually warships powered by banks of oars.

Charts and compasses existed at the time but we do not know if they were used in the smaller vessels Martoni sailed on. Navigation would have depended on the local knowledge and experience of the skipper. On several occasions they wait until nightfall to set sail. This may have been to avoid being seen by pirates or to navigate by the stars or both.

Times of day

In general Martoni's times of day follow the sun - dawn, sunrise, noon, sunset, evening, dusk, night. Vespers was the only liturgical term Martoni uses.

Vespers is usually timed to end at sunset so I have translated it as 'late afternoon'. In addition he mentions the third and ninth hour of the day, and the second and fifth hour of the night. The day between sunrise and sunset was divided into twelve hours. (In winter, daylight hours were therefore shorter than in summer.) Sunrise was the beginning of the first hour. Noon was the sixth hour. So the third hour was mid-morning, the ninth hour mid-afternoon, which is how I translated them. Night was similarly divided, starting at sunset, but unless there was access to a time-keeping device it was hard to be precise.

Meals

There were two main meals. *Prandium* was the first and main meal taken in monasteries after mid-morning prayer. Brunch is the closest equivalent but I decided against nineteenth century Oxford slang in favour of 'morning meal.' *Cena,* the second and secondary meal, often based on left-overs, was eaten after vespers, around sunset. 'Dinner' and 'supper' and 'tea' are ambiguous so I used 'evening meal'. Although he was away for two Christmases and an Easter, Martoni only mentions one festive meal celebrated by the travellers. *Carnisprivio* was the pre-Lent, carnival meal on Shrove Monday and Tuesday.

Money

Ducats are gold coins named after the dukedom of Roger II of Sicily in 1194. By Martoni's time they were chiefly issued by Venice and were one of the principal instruments of international trade. They weighed about 3.5 grammes. Martoni records spending fifty ducats on journeys after he reached Alexandria. The voyages from Gaeta to Egypt, Beirut to Famagusta and some shorter journeys on land are unaccounted for. If he left home with something more than a hundred ducats for travel and living expenses his purse would have weighed not much more than half a kilo, about a pound. He also spends a perperis, better known as a bezant, named after Byzantium, whose coinage it was. He also mentions the carleno, a silver coin issued in Naples, and the bronze granum, a smaller denomination.

Measurement

The most common units of measurement of length in the journal are milearius, canna, pes and palma. I have used miles for milearia. Although the Latin mile is probably longer, Martoni's distances were only approximate. A palma, a hand, is about two inches shorter than a pes, a foot, I turned both into feet, a foot being about thirty centimetres. The canna is eight palms, about eighty inches. I converted them into feet or yards. A yard is about a metre. Other measures of distance are the bowshot, very approximately three hundred yards, and the catapult shot, which I have left.

Areas are the medium terre and the modio. A medium terre is the size of field a team of two oxen could plough in a day. I translated this as acre, which has a similar origin. A modio is a measure of seed, very approximately fifty-five kilos. Originally a modio of land is the area that would require a modio of seed, possibly about a sixth of an acre.

JOHN MOLE

Nicola de Martoni

Lawyer

Pilgrimage to the Holy Places

I

FROM GAETA TO ALEXANDRIA

On the 17th of June 1394, on the eve of Corpus Christi, I, Nicola de Martoni, a lawyer from the town of Carinola, wishing to visit the Holy Sepulchre of our Lord Jesus Christ and other places overseas, embarked with the noblemen Sir Antonatio de Aspello, from Suessa, and Sir Cobello de Dyano, from Teano, and many other pilgrims, on a ship of Mellus Maltacia, from Gaeta, along with four other ships bound for Alexandria, on the way to the holy city of Jerusalem.

On Thursday, the Feast of Corpus Christi, there was a violent storm with gale force winds and heavy seas. We passed the island of Ventotene *(Ventutera)*, about thirty miles from Gaeta. It is six miles in circumference and there is an abundance of fish which attracts fishermen from Ischia and Gaeta.

On Saturday 20 June to sunset on the Tuesday all we saw was sky and sea. The sea was very rough and waves swept over the deck of the ship. As the sun went down on Tuesday all the pilgrims and sailors saw the mountains of Sicily, except me, because of my bad eyesight.

On Wednesday, the Feast of John the Baptist, the sea grew calm and we headed for the island of Marettimo, which is near the town of Trapani. I could see it clearly as it looked like a high mountain, like the Massique in Carinola.

The island of Pantelleria

Heading towards Sicily, the island of Pantelleria is to the north. It is twenty miles in circumference and populated by Saracens, although it is now under Genoese control. *(Saracen was the late Roman and Greek name for Arab and subsequently Muslim.)*

The island of Gozo (Gocze)

On Friday 26 June, towards evening, we came to the island of Gozo, which is about thirty miles round. It is ruled by Artale Alagona of Aragon. There is a castle with about forty dwellings. They have vines and an abundance of silk worms and cumin and all sorts of meat. You can get ten kilos of beef for a carleno. A goat costs four grana and a kilo of lamb two grana.

The island of Malta (Mante)

Three miles from Gozo is the island of Malta, sixty miles around, also ruled by Artale Alagona. There is only one town and several with villages numbering four thousand dwellings. There is plenty of everything they need, as on Gozo. We could see the mountains of Sicily sixty miles away. For a long time we steered clear of them, for fear of the ships and galleys of the Catalans, who were laying siege to the Sicilian town of Catania.

On Friday 26 June we left Malta and Gozo and took to the high seas. Three Genoese ships, one of which had a Genoese captain, left us without warning and headed off to Alexandria. We remained in fear of Catalan ships and for eight days we saw only the sky and the sea.

Methoni and Koroni (Modona et Corona)

On the following Friday, 3 July, towards evening, the mountains of the island of Sapienza came into view. There is nothing there except a castle on the heights protecting Koroni and Methoni three miles away. Koroni is forty miles on from Methoni. They are under Venetian rule. In the past they belonged to our King of Italy, who gave them to the Venetians in return for patrolling the sea to protect the lines of supply to the rest of the Morea from Saracen raids. The Venetians used this pretext to keep control of the territory.

At dawn on Sunday, 5 July, near the island of Kythira, we came across four ships sailing six miles away. We all got our weapons ready for fear they were pirate ships. But they changed direction and headed west.

The Island of Kythira (Citrini)

Kythira lies ten miles from a mountain called Cape Maleas (Capud Sancti Angeli) on the mainland at the southernmost point of the Peloponnese. A hermit lives in a church on the mountain. On Kythira is a city governed by the Venetians.

It was on Kythira that Paris, son of the Trojan king Priam, landed when he came to take back Priam's sister Hesione, who had been abducted by the Greeks. This was against the wishes of Hector and his other brothers, who predicted the destruction of Troy. Paris left for Greece with several ships and landed on Kythira, where there was a temple that stands to this day. Helen, the wife of King Menelaus, who reigned over this part of the Morea, which was then Greece, came to the temple. She was a jewel among women for her beauty. As soon as they saw each other Queen Helen and Paris fell passionately in love. He abducted her from the temple and took her away to Troy.

Let us leave this story to the scholars and students of Troy. The island is very fertile and you get seven crustati to the ducat.

The Islands of Ovo, As and Patas. (Ova, Assi et Patassi)

Between two and four miles away from Kythira are three little islands. One is called Ovo, which is about a mile round, but does not look to me any bigger than the Castell dell'Ovo of Naples. The other islands are called As and Patas. They seem about the same size as Ovo. None of them are inhabited.

The Storm

I should also add that on Monday 6 July after our morning meal, a headwind sprang up that the sailors call the Borea. It blew up a sudden storm with such heavy seas that the sail and the mast seemed to plunge into the depths of the water. I was terrified by the sight and went by myself to a quiet corner of the ship's stern where I wept bitterly, the tears pouring down my cheeks. Weeping for the error of my ways and seeing all the sailors terrified, I begged God to have pity on my sins and to receive my soul that I commended to him. The storm lasted three hours and blew us back forty miles. We decided to land back on Kythira, which we had just left, and to stay there all through Thursday 9 July.

The islands of the Archipelago

On Friday 10 July we sailed between the island of Milos and other islands at the head of the Archipelago. To the south of Milos is the island of Crete *(Candia)*, which is six hundred miles round, and has good wine. It is ruled by the Venetians. Crete can equip sixteen galleys whenever it wants and has the Labyrinth where the Minotaur lived.

Then we came to the island of Christiani *(Sancti Georgii)*, which is uninhabited, and then Santorini, which is twenty miles in circumference and inhabited, and belongs to the Archipelago. The Archipelago is a dukedom consisting of more than three hundred islands, inhabited and uninhabited. The Duke of the Archipelago was killed, leaving his mother to rule some of the islands and the Venetians the rest. All the islands once belonged to Greece and all their inhabitants are Greek. One of them is Chios *(Ssiu)* where they harvest mastic. It is found nowhere else and they sell large quantities for an annual revenue of about fifteen thousand ducats.

The island of Astypalaea (Stampalea)

On Saturday 11 July we sailed by the island of Astypalaea. It is thirty miles round and was inhabited until laid waste by the Turks. Only a castle and its walls can be see. Wild animals live on the island, including goats and asses.

On Sunday 12 July, before the morning meal, we sailed between many inhabited and uninhabited islands, between one and five miles apart from each other.

The island of Kos

Kos *(Lango)* is inhabited. It is two hundred miles round with many castles and houses and belongs to the Knights of Rhodes *(also known as the Hospitallers or the Order of St John of Jerusalem)*. Fifteen miles from the island is the mainland of Turkey *(Torchia)* whose mountains are as high as Mount Marsico.

The island of Nisyros (Niczari)

Two miles from Kos we passed the island of Nisyros. It is eighteen miles in circumference and looks like the Rochetta and Falciono mountains around Carinola. There are three castles, one on the coast and the others on top of the mountain. It has many villages and an abundance of fruit, although they grow no wheat, only barley. The Knights of Rhodes rule the island now but it belonged before to Lord Antonius Assanti of Ischia. He acquired it in the following way. He was on galley with a raiding party and captured a Turkish galley with a pasha on board. He received the island of Nisyros as ransom. He was Lord of the island until his death, when his son succeeded. The son lived on the island until he died of natural causes and the Knights of Rhodes took over. They say that Fra' Dominic de Alemania, who is also a Superior and a Procurator of Rhodes, receives two thousand ducats worth of dried figs every year, so great is the island's fig production.

As we were two miles from the island, six Greeks came from the castle in their boat and came aboard our ship. They looked round and had plenty to drink, promising to come back with fresh meat, grapes and melons, which we were very eager to buy. But they never came back.

The island of Symi (Ssimie)

After Kos we came to the island of Symi which has, so they say, the best wines in the world. They keep these wines in earthenware jars as they don't have casks or the wood to make them. The Knights of Rhodes rule the island. Every day the island sends great quantities of grapes to market in Rhodes. They are very good and cheap. We ate a lot while we were there.

Rhodes (Rodi)

On Monday 13 July before mid-morning we arrived on Rhodes. It would take a long time to describe it but in brief it seemed to me about the size of Capua. The upper city, with the castle and the church of St John, is separated from the lower town by high walls and high, solid towers.

The lower town

The lower town is enclosed by high walls. More people live here than in the upper city. There are shops and grocers and other merchants and it is close to the sea.

The windmills

The port is fairly good and has an excellent mole with ships from all parts. On the quay are fifteen mills, which are powered by the wind. Their construction is impossible to describe in words without drawing a picture. They are about twenty feet apart.

The gardens

All round the city are gardens with orange trees, lemon trees and all sorts of other fruits. Every garden has a large well and a windmill that draws the water with a wheel fitted with buckets. The water runs down a channel into a big tank like a wine press that, when it is full, waters the garden in the evening.

I have to say that in my opinion they are the loveliest gardens in the world. In every one there is a mansion and other houses and in some there are beautiful guest houses with rooms and chambers fit for a count. There are so many gardens that I think they extend three or four miles around the city.

The good climate

In addition I would say the city has an excellent climate and I have never seen so many old men with long beards aged between eighty and a hundred and twenty. In fact I saw more old men than young in the squares.

The priests

The people of the island are Greeks and follow the Greek religion. The clerics, who are called papas, all have beards and their long hair tied up and wear tall broad hats without hoods. They only marry virgins and the lay people are very happy to give their daughters to them. They are all Christians in the town. The main church is the cathedral and is quite sumptuous.

The church of St John of Rhodes

The church of St John is inside the castle and although small is highly venerated. It is said that that it houses many relics, including a cross made from the bowl that Our Lord Jesus Christ used when he washed the feet of the disciples. Two other crosses were made from the same bowl and they are in other churches. There is also a thorn from Christ's crown of thorns. I will describe the relics in detail later as I saw them all on my way back.

The Inn of the Grand Master

Inside the castle is a great inn with many large rooms and chambers where the brothers live, among which are beautiful and highly decorated rooms for the Grand Master of the order when he is in residence. There is also a hostel for pilgrims and the sick, including a large infirmary with doctors always on duty and everything else necessary for the patients.

The church of St Antony

Outside the castle is the church of St Antony belonging to the order of St John, a vaulted building with a large courtyard unique of its kind and closed with a gate. Inside the walls are fifty-one tombs, vaulted and arched like those in St Mathew of Caleno, in which only the brothers of the order are buried. Nobles and soldiers are buried in the church of St John of Rhodes. Others are buried in St Antony's according to their last wishes. But most of the brothers are buried in these tombs, since they bestow absolution of sin and punishment, even to deathbed penitents.

Saint Antony and his miracle

In the church of Saint Antony there is a statue of the saint famous for a miracle. Possessed by the devil, a man struck it in the face with a spear - the wound is visible to this day. He immediately flared up with St

Antony's fire, burning his body as if it was wood. The poor sinner, seeing himself on fire, threw himself into the sea nearby but the more he plunged in, the more he burned until he was entirely consumed. The metal of the spear hangs in front of the blessed statue and there are many silver icons and offerings of ships and food in the church.

The church of St Nicholas and a statue

At the end of the mole is the church of St Nicholas. I was reliably told of a great wonder. In ancient times there was an statue so incredibly enormous that one foot stood at the end of the mole, where the church is, and the other half a mile away at the end of the mole with the windmills. The statue stood square and upright and was so tall that, however big they were, ships could come into the harbour between the legs of the statue with their masts and sails up. From the top of the statue you could see a hundred miles, it was so big. Later it was destroyed.

The name of the statue

The statue was called the Colossus, which is why the people of the island, to whom St Paul sent so many letters to convert them to the holy Catholic faith, are called Colossians, after the statue. *(In fact they are from Colossae in Asia Minor).*

There is nothing more to say about Rhodes. On the evening of Sunday 18 July we left the island and set sail for Alexandria

II

DESCRIPTION OF EGYPT

Alexandria

In the middle of the morning on Friday 25 July we arrived at the port of Alexandria, where there were already ten ships. As soon as we docked, four Saracens came up carrying pigeons. They asked where our ships came from and what they were carrying. One of them immediately wrote a short note and fixed it to a wing of one of the pigeons. He released it and it flew first to the Emir of Alexandria and then to the Sultan in Cairo. The Saracens do this with any big vessel that comes into Alexandria. I witnessed it several times when vessels came into port.

The ports

Alexandria has two harbours. The first, in which we moored, is for Christian vessels. As far as I could see it large and circular and three miles round. It is a bowshot from the city gate. The second port is on the other side, the South, where Christian vessels are not allowed to dock but only Saracen. The reason is that from this harbour the city was captured by the King of Cyprus, Peter I, in 1365. I was shown the extent of the damage done by his army. I estimate that an eighth of the city was destroyed.

The gates

The city gate for Christians is big, I reckon about thirteen feet wide and twenty high. Inside the first gate is a high vaulted passage about twenty yards long leading to a second gate. Both gates are reinforced with iron plates.

The guards

In the passage between the two gates several armed sentries wait on either side. Whenever a Christian goes through they immediately stop him and search him thoroughly all over to see if he has any gold. Pilgrims pay a tax of two ducats for every hundred they bring into the city. Merchants pay a ducat for every ten. A Christian going through the door is searched down to his underwear.

The inns

The city has inns for Christians from the Kingdom of Italy as well as Genoese, Venetians, Catalans and citizens of other Christian kingdoms of the world. A consul resides in each inn, whose job is to look after all his countrymen and hear their complaints.

The different races and their costumes

There are three different races in the city. Saracens wear white linen kaftans and strips of white linen wound several times round their heads. The strips are fifty to sixty arm-lengths long.

Jewish costume

Jews also wear a white kaftan and headgear tied in the same way, except it is yellow.

Copts (Christiani de centura - Christians of the Belt)

Copts also wear white kaftans and the same head-dress, except theirs is blue. They are good Christians who believe in God the Father, The Son and the Holy Spirit and worship the three in one and believe in the blessed and glorious Virgin Mary and other saints. Some of them come from the East and believe in the same things and have their own churches decorated with paintings of saints in which they celebrate mass in their own way.

Reason for the differences in headgear

The variation in headdress started when the city was captured by the King of Cyprus. As a result, Jews and Copts began to wear hats on their heads and other Christian clothes, while the Saracens wanted to wear a different costume.

Size of the city and its population

It is generally considered that the city is bigger than Naples but it does not have beautiful houses. It has more inhabitants than you can count. At any time of day the streets are so crowded that you cannot walk a step without bumping into people.

The main streets

The main streets are full of people and very long, between one and three miles. You can find every trade under the sun. There is one street where they sell gold and silk cloth and is canopied for a mile with embroidered awnings. There are so many sheets of cloth a kingdom could hardly buy them all.

St Catherine's Prison

Inside the city is the prison where St Catherine was held. It is like a small vault. Two tall, broad columns on either side of the street are where Catherine was tied and whipped. There is a little hole in the wall through which the angel of God and Our Lord Jesus Christ brought food for the virgin saint. A great miracle is told about the hole. Several times it was closed up and plastered over but always opened up again

Wine and fruit

The city has excellent grapes. Figs and other fruit are not good. The Saracens do not drink wine and they do not want the Christians to bring it in either, but the Emir graciously allows the consuls to buy one barrel a year. It is very expensive.

Women's Costume

Saracen women wear white kaftans and a white linen cloak over their heads and cover their faces up to the eyes. Saracen men and women are mostly black with some half black. I think fewer than ten out of a hundred are white.

The city walls

The walls are excellent with many towers on the ramparts and in the barbicans. Many of the towers have catapults. Throughout the city there are many stands of date palms of middling height that produce abundant fruit. But when we were there in the last week of July, the dates were not ripe enough to eat.

The hills of Alexandria

There are two artificial hills made of mud and excrement from the streets and houses. They are about two miles apart. On top of one of them, which is higher than the hill of the Holy Archangel of Carinola, is a tower. As the hill grows with mud and excrement, the tower gets higher. This is deliberate so that sailors can spy the city from far away, as it is built on low, flat ground.

Leaving Alexandria

After the morning meal on Sunday 9 August we left Alexandria with fifty four Flemings *(Frandanisi)* among whom were four knights. One of them was a landed knight with twenty men from his household. Some of them were nobles and all were fine young men, none older than thirty. We paid thirty-four ducats each and assembled in front of the Lopepe gate. We went through very nervous of being searched for money, because of the two percent tax on anything coming into Alexandria.

That day we got as far as a little river called the Calese, a mile and a half from Alexandria.

The River Calese

The Calese is a branch of a big river called the Tigris, which flows past Cairo. *(He confuses Babylon, twin city of Cairo, with Babylon of Mesopotamia, whose river is the Tigris).* At the beginning of August every year the Calese has very little water. It grows every day drop by drop until the stream is strong enough to flow through fixed channels to the city of Alexandria and fill up the cisterns. As soon as one cistern is full the water goes underground to the next, in the same way that the wells of the town of Teano are filled. When all the cisterns are full the water is drawn. There is enough for Alexandria for the whole year and is excellent drinking water. Indeed my companions and I drank so much during our seventeen days in Alexandria and at all hours of the day, that I think if it had been Carinola or Teano water, it would have killed us because of the extreme heat. *(Tepid water was thought less injurious than cold).* But as soon as we drank it, we sweated it out. We put three parts water into our wine because it was a good Cretan wine and expensive.

The cisterns and fields: how they are filled and irrigated

Once the cisterns are full, the fields of Alexandria are irrigated through pipes and channels. The fields are flooded for forty days to a depth of about six feet, more or less according to the slope and the height of the sites. After forty days the water is drained off and the Saracens sow the fields.

Delayed at the Calese

We waited at the Calese from Sunday to Tuesday 11 August. We had anxious days and nights waiting for a letter from the Emir of Alexandria notifying the Emir of Cairo of our arrival. We were worried that the letter would not arrive on account of the hostility of the Emir, who is most unjust and is hated by all the Alexandrians and his subjects.

Leaving the Calese

On Tuesday our guide Santaacha, who was to take us to Saint Catherine, arrived with the letter from the Emir. We took to the river with our belongings on three little boats and set off for Cairo.

Gardens

For three miles on both sides of the river we passed large gardens planted with date and cinnamon and other fruit trees and with many Saracen farmhouses on the banks. There were so many palms that it looked like the San Lorenzo forest on the way to Capua.

The Calese

The Calese runs for six months before it dries up and does not return until the following August. This happens every year. The Saracens say that the water flows from Earthly Paradise which is why it is so good.

The villages by the river

The whole day we went past villages crowded along the river. The Saracens' houses are like round bread ovens. There were a great many boys and girls on the bank begging for bread in their language, they are so poor.

In great danger from shipwreck

The following night we stayed on the boats and slept. We were worn out by the intense heat and needed to rest. We went to sleep, fully dressed. At around midnight we had an accident that put us in mortal danger. Our boat was heading towards another one when the steersman at the oar made a mistake and collided with a wall on the bank. The hull was holed and water poured in. Our guide immediately woke us up shouting "get up, get up pilgrims and jump into the water! Get out of the river or we shall all perish." God, the help and support of all those in trouble, willed that the boat, before it sank, ran aground on a little island. Terrified, we got out, but all our bags and beds were in the water. We struggled to get our beds back but lost our baggage and our hardtack and remained all night on the island.

The guide arrives

On the morning of the next day, Wednesday 12 August, our guide Santaacha came back to us. He had gone ahead with the Flemings on another boat. He picked us up along with our beds, clothes and other things, all soaked. We got into his boat and sailed the whole day in intense heat without anything to eat. The river water was our meat and drink. We landed that evening at a village where I went nervously with one of the men to buy food.

Fouah (Fuge)

On Wednesday evening we arrived at a large village or town called Fouah, a dependency of Alexandria. At the port we came to the main river, the Tigris, an expanse of water surrounding an island a hundred miles around. On the island are many other estates and large villages. They say that the island brings in thirteen thousand ducats a year to the Emir of Alexandria.

The Island of Gold

Opposite this island is another belonging to the Emir of Alexandria, about five miles round. It is planted with alfalfa, cinnamon, and many other crops. Its name is Gold Island and brings in fifty thousand bezants a year to the Emir.

The gardens of Fouah and their irrigation

Fouah has the most beautiful gardens in the world, with oranges, lemons, apricots and other fruits. They are very big and the trees are so close together that the sun hardly gets through and nor can you ride a horse through them. The gardens are irrigated all day with water drawn by oxen driving a wheel that raises water into reservoirs and from there through channels in such a way that is impossible to describe without drawing. The oxen work day and night, two or three for each wheel. When one is tired they unharness it to eat and another is attached to the wheel.

Fine-looking oxen

The oxen are big and handsome and are not castrated, so they are stronger. I think they would be worth thirty ducats in our country, more or less, but in this part of Egypt the finest would hardly fetch eight or less.

Enjoying the gardens

We stayed a few days in the gardens, eating and sleeping as long as we pleased in the shade of the fruit trees. The water drawn by the oxen and flowing day and night through the gardens was delightful.

Terrified on the river

Going into the town of Fouah by river we were very nervous because of the strong currents merging around the island and of the words of our guide. "Pilgrims, we are in great danger here." Some of the pilgrims who knew how to swim got ready to do so if necessary but I, wretched and miserable, thought of nothing but death and prayed to God to forgive my sins.

Herds of camels and other animals

All along the river we saw a lot of big camels, buffalos, goats, and cattle drinking on the bank. The buffalo are not as big as those of the Terra di Lavoro. Wild camels congregate in herds like other animals.

Resting

After the morning meal on Sunday 16 August we came to a town beside the river. Because of the extreme heat we rested in the shade of thorn trees, like those the crown was made of to put on the head of Our Lord Jesus Christ as he hung on the cross for our salvation. They are as tall as willows. We stayed there until evening and bought food from the Saracens.

Windstorm

In late afternoon we got back in the boat. While we were on the river a wind came up so strong that it blew up sand from the banks and the land beyond in such quantities that we could hardly see each other or the sky. The storm lasted until sunset and we were terrified.

Damietta and the capture of Saint Louis of France

On Monday we came to an island on which stands the town of Damietta, which belongs to Alexandria. It is said that St Louis of France, inspired by a divine command, landed on the island with a great army to fight the Saracens. While they were there, the Saracens, by some secret method, caused the river to flood the island. Many of the men were drowned and St Louis was taken prisoner. It is said that he was ransomed for so much money that there was hardly any gold or silver left in the Kingdom of France.

The number of towns

It is three hundred miles from Alexandria to Cairo. The river banks are packed with villages one to three miles apart. It said there are seventeen hundred villages, not including the estates and villages in the provinces inland, which are said to number three thousand.

The size of the river and the snake called a cockatrice

The river is quite wide, in some places half a mile, more or less, and has three hundred branches flowing off into the fields and villages of nearby provinces. The river waters the whole land, otherwise sowing crops and harvesting fruit would be impossible, for it only rains once every four years.

In the river live serpents with four legs, called cockatrices. They are so big they sometimes catch and eat oxen and other large animals going down to the river. I did not see any in the river but in Saint Catherine's desert saw lots of similar snakes with legs, although not as big.

The town of Cairo

At sunset on Tuesday we arrived at the city of Cairo, which stretches a a long way along the river bank. It has very beautiful houses with balconies, glazed windows, lattice screens, other fine features, and beautiful gardens behind them. These houses are much more beautiful than the houses on the sea front in Naples, although not so big. The town, including the settlements along the Babylon river, is about thirty miles long.

The number of boats

On the banks of the river I reckon we saw more than two thousand boats bringing food to the people of Cairo, in addition to other boats coming and going into the city. It is remarkable how the world can feed as many people as are in Cairo and Babylon. No-one would think it possible unless they saw it for themselves.

Babylon (Babillonia)

On Wednesday morning we left this part of the river and headed up along the bank to the city of Babylon. We came to a branch of the river that runs between Cairo and Babylon and followed it into Babylon. It is ten miles long with the same very beautiful houses and countless boats all along the shore.

The islands

In front of Babylon are two islands in the middle of the river with beautiful houses and gardens on the banks. As far as I could see one of them is a mile long and the other two.

The house where we stayed

On that day we loaded our baggage on camels and went to the excellent house of the consul, where we stayed while our guide went in search of camels to carry water for us pilgrims and the animals, along with our hardtack, barley for the animals, and other things we needed for St Catherine's desert.

The capture of Babylon

On Thursday 20 August we wanted to see for ourselves the Coptic churches of Babylon and the relics of the saints they contained. We got up early and, with an Italian who was fluent in the language, Antonio Zocto of Florence, we went into Babylon. Much of it was in ruins, dating from the time when his excellency Lord Geoffrey de Bouillon of France, of happy memory, captured Cairo. Wishing to take

Babylon, he laid siege for a long time and when he failed to take the castle destroyed many of the houses and buildings around it.

Walking round the streets of Babylon, they felt like the streets and houses of Rome.

Babylon castle

That day we found the place where the castle stood. It was obviously a big and impressive building before it was destroyed. Now it is the site of many Saracen houses.

The church of St Mary of the Cave

Then we came to the church of St Mary of the Cave, a beautiful church with paintings of Our Lord Jesus Christ, the Blessed Virgin Mary and other saints. We went down underneath to the cave where the Blessed Virgin Mary and her son hid for fear of Herod. Joseph, into whose charge they had been given, was told by the angel of the Lord: "Joseph, Joseph, take the boy and Mary, his mother, and flee into Egypt etc." In this church those who are truly repentant and confess are granted a plenary indulgence.

The church of St Barbara

Then we went to the church of St Barbara, a beautiful church with icons and paintings of the saints and the body of St Barbara, which we venerated. A plenary indulgence is associated with the church.

The church of St Martin and St Barbasus

We then went to St Martin's, a fine church with icons and paintings of the saints. It houses the blessed body of St Barbasus, who is said to have lived in a village of Babylon. He professed his faith in Our Lord Jesus Christ and converted many unbelievers and came to the attention of the Sultan of Babylon, who had him arrested and executed, steadfast in faith. They say he is responsible for many miracles. He died one thousand one hundred and twenty years ago.

The Patriarch

It is worth noting that St Martin's church is the home of the Patriarch. He is regarded as a most holy man and rules the patriarchate as the Pope rules Christendom. He is said to be more powerful than the Pope as his authority extends over a greater part of the world, namely all the countries of Greater and Lesser India.

As we heard much about the Patriarch's sanctity we asked our Christian interpreter to introduce us to him so we could talk with him and discuss what was said about him. Going up through several rooms we first met many pilgrims from India, who had visited the Holy Land of Jerusalem and then came to Babylon to visit the churches and holy places and the holy man, the Patriarch. They wore nothing but a robe and their faces were emaciated and pale from extreme fasting and the trials of travelling from their distant countries. We encouraged them greatly by talking with them about the deeds of God.

After talking with the Indians we went up to where the Patriarch received pilgrims. It was a handsome room with a marble floor covered in carpets. While we were there one of his servants, who were all dressed in robes, went to announce our arrival to the Patriarch. He came in carrying a cross like a prophet with a beard and a saintly expression.

We genuflected and kissed first the ground. then his feet and his bare hands, as he always goes barefoot carrying a cross. He sat down on the carpet and we all sat down in front of him, discussing with him for two hours the deeds of Christ and the saints, our journey and our pilgrimage. He took out balsam and put some on our hands. He presented us with two little flasks of it, asking us for the love of God kindly to accept them as he himself receives it for nothing several times a year from the Sultan, who holds him in high regard, so it is said, for his sanctity.

The Patriarch and the meal we shared with him

After our audience the Patriarch invited us through our interpreter Antonio, since we could not understand the Patriarch or he us, to join him in a meal with a loaf of bread each. We signalled our grateful acceptance and he had his servants bring a wool tablecloth and spread it on the floor. On it they put bread, saucers of honey, big dishes of grapes, figs, peaches, and fried cheese. The Patriarch said grace and invited us to eat. So we set to on the honey and other things. He had hardly eaten a thing when he got up and left, telling us to carry on eating, and went back to his room where he prays and sleeps on the floor at night. We ate and drank the excellent water, as they never drink wine there, only water. At the end of the meal the Patriarch came back and received our thanks for his charity, holding out the cross that he always carries. We all kissed the cross and then his feet, despite his reluctance, and his hand with his permission, and took our leave with his blessing and encouragement.

The Patriarch's works of charity

The Patriarch has so much money coming in from the patriarchate's assets, that we are reliably informed he gets ten thousand ducats a day. After taking out what he and his household needs to live, he gives to the poor and the pilgrims constantly coming to him from India and other parts of the world. He also uses it to support the many people in the large hospice he funds in Babylon. He pays off the debts of Christian debtors detained by the Saracens because he fears that without the means to settle they might renege on the Christian faith and convert to the Saracen religion

Way of life of the Patriarch and his household

The Patriarch and all his household live a life of poverty, making three fasts of forty days a year and never eating meat or fish

The miracle of St Thomas of India

The Patriarch and the Indian pilgrims told us of the great miracle of Saint Thomas the Apostle. His remains are in India on an island surrounded by sea. Every year on his feast day the waters part to allow a great number of Christians from India and other parts of the world to visit the saint without getting their feet wet. Also on his feast day the saint by a miracle puts his arm out of the tomb where he lies and keeps it there. When the Christians go to visit his remains he grabs a priest and does not let him go for the rest of the day. The priest has to stay and say mass at the same spot for the rest of the year and when the saint's feast day comes round again he dies. Then St Thomas catches another priest among the visitors, who has to stay for the rest of the year, and so on every year. In the evening of the feast day when the Christians have gone back to the mainland, the sea goes back to normal.

An audience with the Sultan's vice-regent

On Saturday 22 August we had an audience with the Sultan's vice-regent in Cairo. He lives in a large palace with a big courtyard in front, crowded with Saracens who come to call. The palace is next to the Cairo castle within the confines of Cairo and Babylon and is an imposing and remarkable building. We then had an interview with the senior scribe who wrote down the names of all the pilgrims and made us swear that we were travelling on pilgrimage and not for any other illicit reason that might be against the Sultan's interest.

This done, our guide took us through many fine streets, full of people, to a house with four elephants. One of them was incredibly big, I guess about the size of four big buffalos, with black hair, tethered with a massive chain. Another was as big as a two year old buffalo, and the other two were yearlings. They were all chained and kept apart. They look just like they are painted.

Where they make bricks

As said before, Cairo and Babylon are not far apart. Between them is a branch of the river, the castle and a large populated area in which they make quantities of bricks. It is where the Chosen People were settled in the time of the Pharaohs and reduced into slavery, making bricks, as the Bible clearly recounts.

The size of Cairo and Babylon

The city of Cairo is forty miles round and the city of Babylon fifteen, as I have been reliably informed. Although the river crosses Cairo and Babylon, the population is so big that every day eight or ten thousand camels bring skins of water to sell. I would not have believed it, if I had not seen for myself every day the amazing sight of so many camels carrying water from the river.

Drinking water for the love of God

In Cairo and Babylon many places throughout the city are endowed by Saracens, who die childless, for jars of water to be given to any passer-by who needs it, for the love of God. With some anxiety I drank from them several times for the streets are long.

An excellent method of hatching chicks in incubators

In Cairo they have a wonderful invention which is so hard to believe I am afraid of being called a liar. I certainly would not write about it if I had not seen it for myself. They build ovens, I don't know how, with walls made of jars all round, and put in hens' eggs, ten or twenty or thirty thousand of them, depending on the size, with a carefully tended slow charcoal fire. Chicks hatch after a few days. They are sold by weight when they are hatched, a quart or half a quart, like corn or barley. This is why there are so many hens in Cairo and Babylon. I have truly seen with my own eyes flocks of hens watched by a shepherd like herds of sheep. There is a lot of trade in poultry in these parts.

Giraffes

On the same Saturday that we saw the elephants and the other things, our guide took us to another house to see six animals called giraffes, a marvellous sight. They have the head of a deer with horns a foot long, a thin neck almost a six feet long, and the feet and legs of an ox, but much longer. The skin is a mosaic of red and white patches. The body is about ten feet high.

Granaries of the Pharaohs

Ten miles outside Babylon are ten granaries, six big and four not so big, built by king Pharaoh at the time when seven years of famine followed seven years of abundance, according to the dream interpreted by Joseph. He was sold into Egypt by his brothers and then rose to greatness and power under king Pharaoh, as the Bible relates. We could not go and see the granaries for fear of the Arabs who were making war on the Saracens and making incursions into the territory of Cairo and Babylon. This was because the Sultan had left Cairo with a great army of two hundred thousand men for Aleppo (*Alep*) to defend his country against Tamerlane, king and master of the Tartars, who marched against the Sultan with five hundred thousand cavalry. So we did not go to see the granaries but, as we saw from a distance and as we were told, they are massive. It is thought that nowhere in the world could they be built today. They were about thirty miles away and looked like hills. They have a squared pointed top like the point of a diamond. *(In fact pyramids).*

Matarea

Early in the morning of Sunday 23 August we went to a place called Matarea, six miles from Cairo, where there is an inn with many rooms belonging to the Patriarch. There is a plentiful spring of excellent water like a well. Our Lord Jesus Christ made the spring and created the water when he was with his mother the Virgin Mary and they had no water to wash his clothes. The water pours from the spring and flows through a pipe to another very beautiful marble fountain. Our Lord Jesus Christ himself was washed here and laid in a niche in a wall next to the fountain - he was a little baby then, even though in essence and power the greatest of creatures. Saracens strip off and with the greatest reverence go into the pool to wash. The water is chest high. The Saracens say that whoever washes in the spring will never catch leprosy or any other unpleasant disease.

The Matarea spring

Saracens who live there told us about a miracle. Water is drawn from the first spring with two wheels turned by oxen and piped to the balsam garden. The whole garden is watered. On every Sabbath of whatever year the oxen are unable and unwilling to turn the wheels and draw the water, even if the Saracens yoke all their animals. Through this miracle and many others we restored many to the faith they had lost.

The balsam garden

On the same day, we went with the knight we mentioned before and about six other people to the balsam garden, diligently and carefully tended by Saracens. After we paid the gardener we first came to a big fig tree in which Our Lady hid with her son when she was frightened that Herod was coming after them. They slipped into a gap in the trunk which immediately closed behind them. When she wanted to come out the gap opened up again, which is why it remains open to this day.

Creation of the Balsam garden.

It is believed that the balsam garden was created when Our Lady Queen of the World and Redeemer of the Human Race, stopped here. Afraid for her beloved son she wept and balsam plants grew from her precious tears. Some tell another story, which to my mind is the true version. When the clothes of Our Lord Jesus Christ were washed in the spring and put out to dry in the sun, the balsam trees suddenly sprang up so the clothes did not have to lie on the ground.

What the balsam trees look like.

We went for a walk in the garden and collected young balsam branches. The trees were young, waist high, and the branches are like those of a young mastic tree except that the leaves are not so big. Balsam is harvested in April and May, the gardeners told us. They make a little cut in the branches, like a vine and the balsam flows out to be collected in cotton. A plenary indulgence is associated with Matarea.

Balsam cannot be produced in other parts of the world.

We were told on good authority that many people in Egypt and elsewhere have tried to transplant balsam branches in other places but they have not flourished or put down roots anywhere else. It is said that it is because they are not watered by the Matarea spring. This is why balsam is not found anywhere in the world but Matarea.

Leaving Cairo

On the evening of Thursday 27 August we left Cairo for St Catherine's desert. Some of the pilgrims boarded a boat on the Cairo river with all our things. The rest of us waited all night on the bank for them and our baggage and our food but they did not arrive until mid-morning, because their boat sank. On Thursday evening we had nothing to eat or drink except river water.

III

THE SINAI DESERT

Water and the death of pilgrims
We walked for five days in the desert over hills and valleys of stones and sand, sometimes across enormous hills made of nothing but sand, in such intense heat and burning sun that no-one who has not experienced it could imagine. But my longing to reach the home of blessed virgin Catherine was so great that I cared little for the heat and believe it was the same for my pilgrim companions. One day we found water and the next day not, sometimes two days we found it and one day not, sometimes one day we found it and two days not. We found water in holes dug by Arabs living in the valleys between the hills. Sometimes the water was good, sometimes bad. Wise pilgrims carried lemon syrup, brown sugar, white sugar and other syrups to put into the bad water, which is what I did myself. As I did not have the chance to buy any on the journey, I bought a good stock of it in Babylon, where, so our guide said, the finest grocers in Egypt are found. Many of the pilgrims did not do this and five handsome young men, noble and rich in their own country, died; one in Babylon, another on a sand mountain called Mount Sabinus, where we buried him in the sand; two at St Catherine's church, whom we left there sick and learned later they had died; and the fifth, the noblest and richest of all, in Jerusalem, before he could enter the Holy Sepulchre. Oh God! What could I think, seeing so many young men dead in the flower of

youth, but that I was going the same way! Twice I had an attack of tertian fever *(malaria)* but thanks be to God and St Catherine I recovered on the day we toiled up the mountains of Sinai and St Catherine, which I will describe in more detail later.

The Red Sea (Mare Rubrum)

On Tuesday 1 September, walking almost the whole night, we came to the Red Sea, where King Pharaoh in pursuit of Moses and the Chosen People was killed along with all his people. Although it is called the Red Sea the water is the same colour as other seas.

The Sultan's spring

On the Monday evening we came to the Sultan's spring. It has the worst water, foul by taste, colour and effect. Many pilgrims drank it and came down with diarrhoea. The spring is near the road and guarded by Saracens.

The spring of Moses

Half a mile from the Red Sea is the spring that Moses, after king Pharaoh and his men had died, conjured up for the People of God, who were in fear and distress from being pursued. The water comes out of the sand in great quantity. We drank it avidly for we were very thirsty from lack of water. It had a disagreeable colour and taste and a laxative effect lasting for several days but is otherwise harmless.

The Arabs

In many parts of the desert we met a lot of Arabs with their wives, households and animals. They move around from place to place and do not have proper houses because they are descendants of Pharaoh and cursed by God. In many places women came to meet us on the road with children in their arms, begging for bread for the love of God.

Where Moses was told by an angel to go and talk to God.

At sunrise on Monday 7 September, high in the mountains, we came to the place where an angel sent by God ordered Moses, who was resting there, to go to Mount Sinai to speak with God himself. Christians and Saracens alike bow down and worship the place.

St Catherine's.

On Tuesday 8 September on the birthday of Our Lady the Virgin Mary, having walked all night across high, stony mountains, the like of which we had not come across before, we arrived before daybreak at the monastery of St Catherine's. Unable to enter at that time we slept in front of the monastery until dawn, when we were let in.

The layout of St Catherine's monastery

The monastery with its church is built in a valley between two mountains a good bowshot apart. Entrance is through a narrow gateway with iron-bound gates and then through more iron gates to the church and buildings with many cells for the abbot and the monks.

The church building

St Catherine's church is much venerated. It looked to me the size of the church in Sessa but with smaller transepts. It is clad in marble, mosaics and many paintings and has the most beautiful icons. There are more lamps burning than I have seen in any other church.

St Mary's chapel

In the monastery there is a beautiful chapel of the Blessed Virgin Mary with a very fine decorated ceiling, where, on the morning of her feast day we heard high mass celebrated by the abbot and his monks. It was the Greek liturgy as they are of the Greek faith under the jurisdiction of the Patriarch of Constantinople. It would take too long to write how they celebrate mass, better to describe it in person.

The number of monks

There are two hundred and forty monks and other workers in the monastery. Each one has a job to do in the church or among the other activities of the monastery.

The beautiful garden

In front of the monastery in the valley between the two mountains is a fine garden planted with many figs, almonds, oranges, olives, apples, pomegranates and many pergolas with different varieties of grape all good for eating. The olives were very fat and there is a big cistern of excellent water. We went into the garden and enjoyed the fruit immensely as we were hungry. The trees are planted in sand between the rocks and it is amazing to see how they grow and bear fruit.

The charitable works of the monastery

The monastery gives so many alms it is astonishing that they have sufficient resources to give so much. They give two loaves a day to every pilgrim and food to a great number of Muslim Arabs and sailors from India. The monastery is two days away from the port, where Indians come from with their goods to sell.

Visit to the holy places of Mount Sinai and Mount St Catherine

On Thursday 10 September, we wished to see the other sacred places of Mount Sinai and the mountains of St Catherine. We started by climbing what are supposed to be seven thousand eight hundred steps up Mount Sinai, but they felt a lot more to me as I struggled up. I had been suffering from malaria for a few days and had an attack the previous evening. But here is a genuine miracle. As I began to climb the rough steps, my legs were heavy as tree trunks and I thought several times "Go back, look, you can't follow the other pilgrims." And with tears I begged Almighty God and St Catherine to give me the strength to carry on to the end, which they granted me.

Church of Saint Mary of the Annunciation

Going up the steps we came first to the church of St Mary of the Annunciation. When the monks of the monastery were forced out by Saracens and were coming down, Our Blessed Lady the Virgin Mary appeared to them and told them to go back to the monastery and never leave it again. As a memorial the church was built here.

Church of Saint Hermit

Continuing up we came to the church of Saint Hermit, inhabited by monks from the monastery.

Afterwards there was a long hike to the summit of Mount Sinai.

Where the Law was given to Moses

Under a massive rock we came to the cave where God summoned Moses and gave him the Law. Moses was so terrified by His splendour and majesty that he hid in the cave. We all went inside one by one with the greatest reverence.

The church of Saint Moses

We went to a church on the summit of Mount Sinai called Saint Moses. It contains many beautiful paintings and is looked after by monks of the monastery.

The church of Saint Mary of the Green Valley and its garden

After our morning meal we came down from Mount Sinai to a valley, in which stands the church of Saint Mary of the Green Valley, inhabited by monks from the monastery. It has a very beautiful garden with many different fruit trees - figs, vines, pears that look and taste like St John pears, plums, peaches, almonds, apples, pomegranates, and pergolas with different kinds of grape. It would have been a beautiful garden in Sorrento or Salerno. We ate the fruit with a will as there was plenty of it and most excellent. When we had eaten and recovered our strength we went up a mountain higher than the others and longer and more difficult to climb. We reached the summit with a great deal of effort and difficulty. In parts the path had collapsed and was unbelievably arduous. Oh, the weary flesh of man, what trials and tribulations you undergo to attain divine grace - and rightly for it is more precious than anything else - the dwelling place of eternal glory, the splendour of the Divine and eternal joy

Where the body of Saint Catherine was brought by the angels
On top of the mountain is the place where the holy angels brought the body of Saint Catherine when she was beheaded in her martyrdom for the love of Christ in the city of Alexandria. For four hundred years her body lay in a shallow cave in solid rock. We came down the mountain with considerable difficulty and returned to Saint Catherine's monastery in the evening.

The relics of Saint Catherine
On the following Friday we venerated the body of Saint Catherine. It lies next to the high altar of the church in a beautiful iron-bound marble sarcophagus.

Leaving the church
After we had venerated the body and made our offerings we admired the handsome chapel in which Moses received the seven tablets from God. We left the church of Saint Catherine with all our baggage and slept that night outside the monastery. On the Saturday we started on our journey to Jerusalem.

Gaza (Gazara)
We walked across the desert over mountains of stone and sand and the great valleys in between, like those through which we came, until, on the evening of Tuesday 23 September, we came to the great town of Gaza. It is bigger than Alexandria in circumference but does not have as many inhabitants or as beautiful houses or ramparts. They have the best fruit of all kinds, especially grapes. It is five miles from the sea.

Leaving Gaza

On Saturday 26 September we left Gaza and put up for the evening in a hostel built by a Saracen, which welcomes free of charge all pilgrims and Saracens staying in the place or passing through. However there are no beds. It is ten miles from Gaza.

The fountain of the twelve apostles and the monastery where Abraham, Isaac and Jacob are buried.

Before midnight on Saturday we left the hostel and headed for Bethlehem. All that night and all of Sunday until sunset we walked through rocky valleys. We came across many springs in which men and animals drink freely. One of them was called the Well of the Holy Apostles. It is beneath a mountain on which stands a Saracen monastery where Abraham, Isaac and Jacob are buried. This is the mountain God showed to Abraham when he wanted to put him to the test, saying "Abraham, take your only son etc." We did not go up the mountain because of the many Saracen horsemen riding up that day, including the Emir of Damascus with a big entourage of cavalry. There are many fine olive groves in the valleys, like those of Gaeta and Maranola, and also vineyards. At sunset we arrived very tired at the church of Our Lady of Bethlehem.

Where Adam the first man was created.

In these mountains is the place where God created Adam, the first man.

The church of Our lady of Bethlehem

The church of Our Lady of Bethlehem was once very big and beautiful before the Saracens destroyed it. It had a big castle and many other large, fine buildings in front of the church, but they are all in ruins. The church is comparable with Capua in size, but not as wide and has aisles on each side. There are forty-four pillars in the nave and aisles. The walls around the church are covered with mosaics, with gold mosaic in the apse around the high altar. In the apse are three images: the Blessed Virgin with her beloved Son in the middle, David on one side and Abraham on the other beside Our Lord, all beautifully worked in gold, like the apse of Saint Bernard of Caleno.

Where Our Lord Jesus Christ was born
    Beneath the high altar are a few steps leading down to a vaulted crypt. It is where the most blessed Virgin Mary gave birth to her beloved son Our Lord Jesus Christ. There is an altar with a most beautiful icon of the Nativity, that gives absolution of sin and remission of punishment. In the same crypt is the place where Our Lord was laid in a manger before the animals. A similar indulgence is associated with it.

Where St Jerome lived
    Under the high altar, reached by steps on the right, is another crypt where St Jerome lived for many years, translating the Bible from Greek into Latin until his death. His tomb is here. The bodies of many of the Holy Innocents, murdered on the orders of Herod, were also laid to rest here. A plenary indulgence is granted.

Where Christ was circumcised
    In this church at the right of the altar is the place where Our Lord Jesus Christ was circumcised, with

41

which a plenary indulgence is associated. The church consists of a beautiful cloister, a refectory and a dormitory, decorated with the finest mosaics. On the long side they depict the three Kings bringing gifts to Our Lord Jesus Christ. There is plenty of water in the church in wells and cisterns.

Bethlehem was a great city but has been in ruins from the time the Christians lost it. There are about thirty miserable hovels where Saracens and Copts live. Bethlehem is built on a hill surrounded by many olive groves.

Where the angel announced the birth of Christ to the shepherds.

Opposite Bethlehem on another little hill about a mile away from the church is the place where the angel announced at night the birth of Christ to the shepherds, saying "I bring you news of great joy, etc."

Leaving Bethlehem

On Sunday 28 September we left the church of the Blessed Virgin Mary in the direction of Jerusalem. After half a mile we came across a large stone monument in which the powerful lady Rachel lived and died. In two miles we arrived at the house of the prophet Elijah and shortly afterwards the place where the star appeared to the three Kings bringing gifts to Our Lord Jesus Christ in Bethlehem.

IV

JERUSALEM

Jerusalem

On the evening of the same day we entered the city of Jerusalem and put up at the hostel where all the pilgrims stay. In the days when the Knights of Saint John held it along with the Holy Sepulchre, the hostel was a grand and remarkable building that had to be seen to be believed. But now it is reduced to a large vaulted building, long and wide, with columns in the middle and several rooms for pilgrims.

Following are all the indulgences of Jerusalem

On Tuesday, the penultimate day of September, wishing to visit the following sacred places outside the Sepulchre, we got up in the middle of the night and, with two Friars Minor, one of whom was the vicar of the Franciscan monasteries, went to the places listed below that grant indulgences, as we were told by the Friars and according to many other texts. Those marked by a sign of the cross + give to those who truly repent and confess plenary absolution of sin and punishment, and the other places marked with a Y grant seven years absolution and seven indulgences of forty days.

- First we came to the gate of Jerusalem. +
- The place where the three Marys met Jesus carrying the cross and wept for overwhelming grief and Jesus said to them "Weep for yourselves etc." Y
- The house where Our Lady the Virgin Mary studied for many years. Y

43

- The place where the Virgin Mary met Christ, her beloved son, carrying the cross to the place of execution, and fell on the ground out of grief. The place is called Our Lady of Sorrows. Y

- The place where the Virgin Mary was born. Y

- The palace of Herod which is no longer intact and which we could not enter. Y

- In the centre of the town are many places associated with indulgences which pilgrims cannot enter, like the Temple of Solomon. From a distance it looks a remarkable building and very beautiful. Or the temple next to the Temple of Solomon, where our Lord was presented in the arms of blessed Simeon. Or the Golden Door which is now closed. There are many other places where pilgrims are not allowed.

- Outside the town is the valley of Josaphat where the Last Judgement will take place. It stretches eight miles from the Mount of Olives and Galilee to the city of Jerusalem and has orchards everywhere. Y

- In the middle of the valley of Josaphat is the place where Saint Stephen was stoned by the Jews. Y

- Beyond the valley of Josaphat is the church where Our Lady the Virgin Mary was buried by the holy apostles. Thirty eight steps go down to it and in the middle is her beautiful tomb with two little doors. **+**

- The place where Our Lord Jesus Christ, knowing that he would undergo death for the salvation of mankind, prayed three times to his Father "Father, if it is possible etc." A crypt stands on the spot where he uttered this prayer and where holy angels comforted him. Y

- Nearby is the place where Christ told his apostles to wait when he went away to pray, saying "Stay here etc." Y

- The place where armed Jews seized Jesus at night at the signal agreed with Judas: "The one whom I kiss will be Jesus, seize him etc."
- The place where the Apostle Peter saw Christ arrested and cut off the ear of the high priest's servant. Y
- Nearby is the place where the Blessed Virgin ascending into heaven threw her belt down to the Apostle Thomas, who had come from India and was not in time for the funeral at her tomb. Y
- The place where Christ, knowing what was going to happen before his most holy passion, wept for Jerusalem. Y
- Then the place where the angel sent from God announced to the Virgin Mary her death and gave her a palm to comfort her. Y
- Mount Galilee where Our Lord Jesus Christ appeared to his disciples after his resurrection. It is beyond the valley of Josaphat half a mile from the Mount of Olives. Y
- The Mount of Olives where Our Lord Jesus Christ, after forty days, ascended into heaven, watched by his disciples. A beautiful church stands here with steps going up to it. In the middle is fine tomb and an altar. **+**
- The place where the Holy Apostles composed the Creed. It was formerly a large dwelling house but now it is in ruins. Y
- Close by is the place where Our Lord Jesus Christ, wishing to teach his disciples how to pray, said "Our Father who art in heaven etc." Y
- The place where Saint James the Less died. Y
- Bethphage where Christ mounted a donkey on palm branches. Y

- Nearby is a fine sepulchre hewn out of a single block of marble forty or fifty feet high, adorned with various beautiful carvings. It was made for the body of Absalom, King David's son, who made war on his his father. King David's men fought him off and pursued him. As Absalom fled, his hair caught in a branch overhanging the road and he was killed. He was not interred in this tomb, although it was made so magnificent for him, but it is supposed to be the tomb of the wife of Solomon, daughter of King Pharaoh. There is no indulgence associated with it.

- Beyond the valley of Josaphat, in a cave down several steps is a spring, where the clothes of Our Lord Jesus Christ were washed. We went down and drank from the spring. The Saracens come in and wash themselves with great devotion. Y

- Further on is the pool of Siloam, where Christ restored the sight of a blind man. After going down there is a kind of cloister that goes round to where the water comes out. We drank it with great devotion. Y

- Near the pool of Siloam is a pillar where the Jews sawed the prophet Isaiah in half. Y

- Going up towards Mount Zion is the cave in which the Holy Apostles hid after the glorious passion of Our Lord Jesus Christ, for fear of Herod who persecuted them. Y

- Close by is the holy ground which was bought for the thirty pieces of silver, the price of Christ, that was given to Judas and which he gave back when he repented of his betrayal. Pilate and the other officials did not want to put the money back in the treasury as it was the blood price of the Just. And so they decided to buy the field as a burial place for pilgrims. It measures about an acre and has many deep pits. They open from the top so the bodies of pilgrims, who have died in Jerusalem, can be thrown in. While we were there many pilgrims had recently been buried. Because of the smell we could not stay to look at the pits. Y

- We then climbed up holy Mount Zion, a mile from Jerusalem and separated from the Mount of Olives by the valley of Josaphat. In former times King David's castle stood on Mount Zion. When Saint Helena came to Jerusalem to requite the death of Christ, she built the church of Saint Mary which now belongs to the Franciscans. She founded many other great buildings in memory of the deeds of God, the Blessed Virgin and other saints. All these buildings are in ruins, utterly destroyed by the Saracens. The places and remains of various occurrences are as follows.

- On Mount Zion is a church with a large, fine nave in which the Franciscans hold their services. Inside, on the high altar, is where Our Lord Jesus Christ gave communion to his disciples. Y

- Next to the high altar on the right is where Our Lord Jesus Christ washed the feet of his disciples. Y

- Outside the church is where the Holy Spirit came down on the Apostles on the day of Pentecost. +

- Close by is a beautiful chapel, where Saint Thomas touched the hands and the side of Christ. +

- Outside the church to the right going out, is where Blessed Virgin Mary remained praying for fourteen years. Y

- Nearby is where Saint Matthew was chosen by the Holy Spirit to be an Apostle. Y

- The place where Saint John the Evangelist celebrated mass in the presence of the Virgin Mary. Y
- The place where the Blessed Virgin Mary left this world. **+**
- The place where Christ preached to his disciples. Y
- The tomb of David and Solomon. Y
- The place where the water was warmed to wash the feet of the disciples and where the lamb was cooked for the Last Supper. Y
- The place where Saint Stephen the First Martyr was buried. Y
- The place where the Jews tried to snatch the body of the Blessed Virgin Mary from the hands of the Apostles as they carried her to her tomb. Y
- Near Mount Zion is the church of the Blessed Saviour that contains the stone that was rolled across the entrance to Christ's tomb. Pilgrims cannot go in as it is occupied by Saracens.

The Holy Sepulchre

On Wednesday, the last day of September, we visited the church of the Holy Sepulchre. About ten yards from the entrance inside the church is a red and black stone the size of a man, on which Our Lord Jesus Christ was laid when he was taken down from the cross and anointed with aromatics. **+**

- Inside the church is the sepulchre of Our Lord Jesus Christ in the middle of the nave in a wonderfully fashioned tomb. First you go into a little room about six feet wide and then through a low door into the Lord's Sacred Sepulchre. There is room for no more than about five men when mass is said inside. **+**

- Above the sepulchre is a large round cupola with a wide opening, like that of Saint Mary of Rome but not as high or wide, I reckon about half the size. After this is the nave with the high altar. On either side are aisles with vaulted ceilings and chapels and beautifully decorated columns. ✛
- In the aisle in front of the chapel of the Blessed Virgin is the round stone where Christ appeared to Saint Mary Magdalen after his glorious passion, dressed as a gardener. Y
- Then you go into the chapel of the Blessed Virgin Mary in which Saint Helena discovered three crosses, one belonging to Our Blessed Saviour and the others to the good and bad thieves. She did not know on which cross hung the saviour of the world, Our Lord Jesus Christ, so she placed a dead man on the three of them in turn. When the body was put on the Lord's cross he came alive, proving that this was the true cross. This is also where an angel said to Mary: "The Lord is risen." This chapel is beautiful and large and has the finest icons. ✛
- Inside the chapel is the pillar where Christ was tied and scourged. It is in a little crypt behind a grille up five steps. Y
- Then the chapel where Our Lord Jesus Christ was imprisoned. Y
- Then the chapel where the Jews divided Our Lord's clothes among them by lot following the prophecy: "My clothes were divided and they drew lots for my coat." Y
- Then a chapel with the pillar to which Our Lord Jesus Christ was tied when he was crowned with thorns. Y

- After this, down thirty marble steps, is the chapel of Saint Helena. Y
- Then the place, down eleven marble steps, where Saint Helena found the Holy Cross and the crosses of the two thieves. The hill used to be here before it was dug out to find the Holy Cross. +
- Then comes the chapel of Calvary, up nineteen marble steps, where Christ was nailed to the cross and sent to his death for the salvation of the human race. Here is the crack in the earth that opened up on the day Our Lord Jesus Christ died. Calvary used to be a small hill where justice was meted out to all those condemned to death. We heard solemn mass in the chapel and the pilgrims received Holy Communion. +
- In the nave of the church is the place where Our Lord Jesus Christ raised his finger and said: "This is the centre of the world." Y
- Next to the chapel of Mount Calvary is a chapel with the head of Adam, the first man. It has two fine tombs, six feet apart, containing the illustrious princes of happy memory King Baldwin and his brother Godfrey of Bouillon of France. They captured the city of Jerusalem and all the other lands of Syria. Y

On the tomb of King Baldwin is carved in verse:

> King Baldwin - the next Judas Maccabeus
> Hope of his country, might of the church,
> Pillar of both
> Feared and brought tribute by all
> Lebanon, Egypt, and murderous Damascus
> Oh woe! - is enclosed in this modest tomb.

On the tomb of Godfrey of Bouillon were carved these words, which I also read:

Here lies Duke Godfrey of Bouillon
Who captured all this land for the Christian faith.
May his soul reign with Christ. Amen.

The church of the Holy Sepulchre, the church of Bethlehem, the church of the Ascension of the Lord, the church of Our Lady's Sepulchre, and many other churches, said to number three hundred and sixty, were founded by Saint Helena to the glory of God, the Blessed Virgin Mary and the saints, to commemorate what happened in Jerusalem at that time. Many of them were for the most part destroyed by the Saracens. There are several buildings and apartments in the church of the Holy Sepulchre, some of which accommodate the Franciscan Brothers, who assiduously celebrate the divine office. The Emir of Jerusalem does not allow some other churches to open. He keeps the keys of the Holy Sepulchre.

On Thursday the first of October, after the pilgrims had heard mass in the Holy Sepulchre and High Mass in the sacred Mount Calvary and received Holy Communion, and made an offering, however much each wished to give, we left the Holy Sepulchre in the evening.

In front of the church of the Holy Sepulchre is a wide square about an acre in size, paved with marble flags. In the middle is the place where Our Lord Jesus Christ, carrying the cross of his passion to come, was exhausted and rested with his cross. Y

Outside the church around this wide paved square are four chapels. One is the chapel of the Blessed Virgin and Saint John the Evangelist. Y. The second is the chapel of the Angels. Y. The third is Saint John the Baptist. Y. And the fourth Saint Mary Magdalen. Y. The entrance to this church is most beautifully worked with various carvings and on the left is a tall and finely decorated bell tower.

On the evening of Friday 2 October we left Jerusalem and headed to the river Jordan. We walked almost the whole night and the following day across rocky mountains and valleys, the going indescribably rough.

The River Jordan

Before sunrise on the following Saturday we came to the river Jordan, in which some of the pilgrims bathed and others did not, as the sun was not up yet. The river is thirty miles from Jerusalem. It looked to me like the river at Castel Volturno but not as wide. +

The Dead Sea where Sodom and Gomorrah were engulfed

Below the river is the Dead Sea where Sodom and Gomorrah and five other cities along with their lands were engulfed on account of the sin of Sodom which they practised among themselves. The sea is about eight days march long and the river Jordan flows into it. Oh what a horrible and foul sin to be shunned by all Christians, to whom God has given female company or wives so that each man should know how to possess his own vessel! Oh how miserable are the men who practice such a foul crime, for the laws oppose and justice takes up arms and the heavenly host is in uproar when such an abominable sin is committed.

The chapel of Saint John the Baptist

Coming back we found the chapel of Saint John the Baptist half a mile from the river. It contains the left hand of Saint John, complete with its flesh. Greek monks occupy the chapel. The entrance is through a massive marble door fitted with a cleverly made iron lock and iron bolts. It is three feet wide and four feet high.

Jericho and Mount Quarantania

We left the river on Saturday and reached Jericho, where there are Saracen houses and beautiful gardens and springs. In the middle of the afternoon we climbed the mountain where Our Lord Jesus Christ fasted forty days and nights. The path is narrow and in very bad repair. In the middle of the mountain are caves whose entrance is through three archways or passages. A little way beyond and higher up is another cave, in which Our Lord Jesus Christ fasted forty days. Saint Helena built a church here. It is associated with a plenary indulgence. +

Bethany

At dawn on the following Sunday we arrived in Bethany at the houses which belonged to Lazarus, the brother of Saint Mary Magdalen and Saint Martha. It was apparently a large structure, like a castle, but is totally ruined except for a vaulted brick building containing a fine marble tomb where Saint Lazarus was buried until Our Lord brought him back to life saying: "Lazarus, come out." Bethany seems to have been a large town but now it is completely destroyed with very few inhabitants. There is absolution. +

The mountain of Judea

On Monday 5 October we came to Mount Hebron and, in a valley, the house of Zachariah where Saint John the Baptist was born. It was apparently a big dwelling, like a castle. It is totally in ruins apart from a chapel under a brick vault, which used to be a beautiful chapel but only two walls remain. In the vault are two altars where the Greek priests who live there say the holy office in the Greek rite. As is the Greek custom they have many books, big and small. On the right of the chapel is a little opening into a cleft in the mountain. When Saint John and some of the Innocents were being pursued by Herod's men he ordered the mountain to open, which it did, and he hid inside with the Innocents. In the habitable part is a large vault, like a courtyard, with massive pillars, where the Greek priests live. Here the disciples of God sang two psalms, *Magnificat animam meam Dominum etc* and *Benedictus Dominus Deus Israel* in praise of the Blessed Virgin Mary. +

Below these dwellings, two bowshots along the road, is a beautiful well of excellent water where Saint Elizabeth greeted the Blessed Virgin Mary coming to meet her. On the other side of the well, a bowshot away, is a large group of handsome buildings, now in ruins, which was the house of Zechariah, the father of Saint John. When he grew up Saint John asked for and received permission from his father to stay there and serve God in prayer. He lived there for some time. One church we could not go into. The Mount Hebron is four miles from Jerusalem.

Where the wood of the Holy Cross grew

On Monday we took another road back and came to a church about a mile from Jerusalem, which Saint

Helena built. It has a fine vault and a number of other buildings. The church is about as wide and long as Carinola's. Under the altar is a big hole where the tree grew that made the Holy Cross on which the saviour of the world hung. Greek priests celebrate the office here in the Greek rite. It is associated with an indulgence. +

The layout of Jerusalem

The city of Jerusalem is extensive and beautiful. All the streets are arcaded and crowded with Saracens. Men and women, Saracens and Copts and Armenians dress and behave as they do in other parts of Syria. In my opinion the city is built on the highest mountains in the world. Jerusalem is surrounded by mountains at least a day's walk away, on which, or in their valleys, there are many vineyards. I think that the whole of the Terra di Lavoro does not have so many vines but they do not make wine. They eat some of the grapes fresh, excellent eating as they grow on rocky ground. The rest they leave to dry on the vine and harvest them to make raisins from which they make wine the Saracen way. They grow next to nothing in the way of food and bring in all their produce from Gaza and other neighbouring areas, from where and by whatever route is at least twenty miles to Jerusalem.

V

FROM JERUSALEM TO JAFFA

Leaving Jerusalem and arriving in Ramla (Rama)

On the night of Wednesday 7 October, after venerating the Holy Sepulchre of Our Lord we left for Ramla, twenty miles from Jerusalem, and arrived in mid-afternoon on Thursday. Ramla is a substantial town but does not have walls. A large number of Saracens live there. It has an inn with rooms where pilgrims stay on their way to the Holy Sepulchre. On the day we arrived in Ramla, Mellus Maltacia, the commander of our ships, also arrived from the port of Jaffa with the pilgrims who stayed with him in Alexandria. I waited for him there while they went to the Holy Sepulchre, having said goodbye to Antonatio and Perreco, who left on a ship to Venice. A shame that I did not go with them! I would not have suffered so many trials and tribulations, as will be seen later. I did not go with them, as I had left my money with the ships when I went to Saint Catherine's and I needed to get it back.

Saint George

On Friday morning we went to Saint George's church, two miles from Ramla, where Saint George was beheaded on a pillar. His body is under the pillar and cannot be seen. The beautiful church was built by Saint Helena but the Saracens destroyed it after the Christians lost Syria and Jerusalem.

Waiting in Ramla and leaving.

I stayed seventeen days in Ramla sick to the stomach with anxiety from being constantly pestered by Saracens asking me in their language: "Why are you staying here so long?" I did not dare go out to buy food, they harassed me so much with spitting and throwing stones and other insults. On 25 October I left Ramla with Mellus Maltacia and the other pilgrims who had come back from the Holy Sepulchre.

Jaffa (Zaffa)

On the same day, 25 October, we arrived at the port of Jaffa. It used to be a great city, built on a hill and was under Pisan rule until the Saracens captured and totally destroyed it so there is not a wall left standing. There are only cellars where the castle had been, in which merchants store the goods they sell in Ramla. Springs with excellent sweet water are only ten yards from the sea

The pillar of Jaffa

In the port of Jaffa is a pillar half three feet high, to which Saint Peter tethered his boat at the time he fished here. The Blessed Virgin Mary sat on it with her beloved son, so reverent pilgrims come and take a stone. From the extent of the drains it is obvious that Jaffa was a big town. The Saracens destroyed it, fearing that it would fall into the hands of the crusaders, since it is the port for the regions of Syria and Jaffa.

VI

FROM JAFFA TO CYPRUS

On 27 October we left the port of Jaffa in a decked ship, for which we payed a ducat and a half per pilgrim. The seven crew constantly argued and quarrelled among themselves. It took five days to get to Beirut. God willed that we had good weather, for otherwise we would have been in danger because of the bad crew. From Jaffa to Beirut is a hundred and sixty miles.

Beirut (Barutum)

On 1 November on the feast of All Saints we got to Beirut in time for mass. The port of Beirut is not very good, especially in winter. It has two towers seven yards apart on either side of the entrance channel, too narrow for all but small boats. The towers are well guarded day and night, especially the taller one. Mellus's ships arrived on the same day as us. He was afraid they were lost because they were twenty-seven days late getting from Jaffa to Beirut, a crossing they should have made in a day given the short distance. But they had run into such a violent storm that two big anchors were lost at sea.

The port

Beirut is the main port for Damascus. It takes two days to bring the merchandise from Damascus to Beirut on animals. The city is small and unattractive. There are many gardens inside and outside the city, where there are also olive groves. Many Venetian and Genoese merchants live there.

Church of Saint Francis

Inside the city is the church of Saint Francis. It used to be a beautiful church when the Christians ruled. Now there is only one vault with an altar where mass is said for the merchants every day. There are other small buildings where the guardians live. There was only one when I was there, living on the charity of the merchants. He is under the guardian or vicar of Mount Sion, who is responsible for all of Syria.

Church of Saint George

Two miles from Beirut is the church of Saint George. In the cave underneath lived the dragon which devoured so many people. Saint George rescued the noble lord's daughter from the dragon's mouth as it was about to eat her. He miraculously tied up the dragon and gave it to the young woman.

The miracle of the church of Saint Francis of Beirut

The guardian of Saint Francis told me of a miracle, attested by many others, that not long ago, while two devout Christians were praying before the crucifix, as was the custom then, two Saracens came in and seeing them praying, took out their knives and stabbed the crucifix. It was painted on a wooden board that suddenly gushed so much blood that the Saracens were soaked in it and ran away. The officers of the town saw them covered in blood and assuming they had murdered someone, arrested them and questioned them. They described the miracle. From that moment on many Saracens seeing this were converted to the Christian faith.

In danger of drowning

Let me tell you what happened to me in Beirut. One day I climbed down from the ship onto a large boat laden with salt belonging to Mellus, that he was taking to a warehouse. I wanted to go ashore to buy provisions. Passing through the channel between the two towers, the sea was so rough it came over the side of the boat before we could get inside the port and the waves came in and swamped us. Not knowing how to swim I thought I was dead. If God, the help of all in despair, had not willed a Saracen to pull me out of the sea, with great difficulty, my life would have been over. It is not surprising that, because of this and many other dangers before and after, my hair and my beard turned prematurely white

Leaving Beirut

I wanted more than anything to get back home. Seeing that Mellus was postponing for too long his departure with his ships, on the night of 24 November, the feast of Saint Catherine, I left Beirut on a ship from Constantinople bound for Famagusta, Cyprus, a voyage of a hundred and sixty miles. I hoped to get a big ship from there to Genoa, which was supposed to leave in a few days.

VII

CYPRUS

Famagusta

I arrived in Famagusta on 27 November. It used to belong to the King of Cyprus, a fine island five hundred miles around. Now the Genoese occupy Famagusta. It is a big city, I think about the size of Capua, and has handsome streets and houses similar to Capua's, but about a third is uninhabited and the houses are in ruins, dating from the time the Genoese took over. The city has finer battlements than I have seen anywhere else, high, with a wide rampart-walk and tall towers all round. They are diligently guarded day and night by the Genoese for fear of the King of Cyprus. There are seven hundred armed soldiers in the pay of the Genoese and keep guard with tight discipline.

The citadel

The citadel is impressive and almost totally surrounded by the sea, apart from a quarter or so on the city side, where the moats are stone clad on both sides and filled with sea water. As a result the citadel is impregnable.

The harbour

Famagusta has a good harbour sheltered on all sides from the wind. In front of one of the city gates is a wooden quay, a stone's throw in length, where vessels tie up and are loaded with merchandise.

The population of the city and the bad climate

The Genoese live in one part of town and the Greeks in a larger part, for the population of the island is Greek. They make a lot of fine camlet cloth *(made of camel or goat hair)*. A law of Famagusta, and of the whole island, is that no woman may leave the city without permission of the Governor or she will be summonsed by his court on her return to the city. Permission is rarely given. The reason apparently is that the men cannot get by without the women spinning and making wool for camlet, as they live on practically nothing else. There is another reason for keeping people in the city, which they are too embarrassed to talk about. The city has the worst climate. The death rate is high at all times of year, more among the Genoese than the Greeks. While I was there, a little over a month, the new Governor, who had arrived from Genoa, died, along with many others. I was afraid all the time I was in the city, especially as I was separated from my companions and had no help or advice as to my personal safety or getting back home.

Church of Saint Nicholas

The cathedral of Famagusta, dedicated to Saint Nicholas, has a handsome nave with many chapels on either side. The bishop is Genoese. In former times, when the city was under the King of Cyprus, he had an annual income of four thousand ducats. I was told that his income is now less than two thousand, as he lost all jurisdiction over the island after the Genoese took the city. I can well believe he is poor for one day, after hearing mass at the cathedral, as I was short of money, I thought I would ask the bishop for charity for the love of God. I went up to him reverently, like a pilgrim and said: "Father, your Excellency, these words are from the bible: I cannot dig, to beg I am ashamed. I ask you as a father to come to the aid of a poor pilgrim with a charitable donation." He replied that he was poorer than I was and swore that he did not have enough to live on himself.

This is where I later attended matins on Christmas Eve, and high mass and the other Christmas services.

The food market

The house where the Governor lives used to belong to the King of Cyprus when he ruled the city. It is quite impressive with a large forecourt, many buildings and a beautiful garden. Between it and Saint Nicholas Cathedral is a large market hall the size of Capua's, selling bread, a lot of oil, and other produce, just like Capua. Every day people sell cloth and many other things. It is in the middle of the city.

The friary of Saint Francis

The friary of Saint Francis in the city has a handsome cloister, a dormitory, many rooms and other apartments, and a fine garden with plenty of water from wells and cisterns. The guardian told me that they have a hard life and do not receive many offerings.

The church of Saint Stephen

The church of Saint Stephen in the city has a hostel, but is poverty stricken at present. I heard high mass in the church on the feast of Saint Stephen and saw his bones and many other holy relics. The church has the finest crucifix I have ever seen, decorated and worked all over with the purest gold.

The monastery of Our Lady of the Wayside

The monastery of Our Lady of the Wayside is in the city. The church is very beautiful and highly venerated with a vaulted nave and chapels on either side, and fine paintings and murals. There is a beautiful cloister, with orange trees and other fruits, and a dormitory and several other houses for the brothers. In the church I saw the following relics:

- The head of Saint Ursula in a beautiful silver case.
- The tibia of Saint Leo, the pope.
- The head of Saint Cufinus
- The head of Saint Sosus
- A fragment of the Holy Cross.

The monastery of Saint Dominic

The monastery of Saint Dominic in the city has a fine church and nave, a beautiful cloister with a garden, a dormitory and other houses for the brothers, although several are in ruins. At present all the friars of Famagusta live very poorly.

The town of Famagusta

Outside the city there used to be a large lower town with a big population. I estimate there were two thousand households, and among them many fine churches. But now the town is totally destroyed, to the extent that there is not a single house intact or anyone living there. The churches include Our Lady of the Grotto, which many worshippers both Latin and Greek visit out of piety.

The layout of Famagusta

Part of Famagusta is on the sea while the greater part is inland and surrounded by excellent moats engineered on both sides. The whole city, including the ramparts, is built on solid marble rock and impossible to excavate. On the sea side is a large and handsome arsenal like that of Naples. In former times, a hundred years ago, the city was founded and built in a place called Constantia, four miles from Famagusta. It was named after King Constus, the father of Saint Catherine, who built it. It was two miles from the sea and did not have a harbour. After Acre was lost, the last town in Syria to be lost by the Christians, all those who escaped fled to the island of Cyprus. It was then that the ancient city of Constantia was transferred to present-day Famagusta.

Women's dress

As a result all women, in Famagusta as well as the rest of the island, wear a black veil over their heads that obscures their faces. The custom derives from the pain and grief of losing Acre and the other towns of Syria. Most of the population of Famagusta came from Acre.

The bad climate

Between Famagusta and the ancient city of Constantia is an extensive marsh that looks like an arm of the sea. They say that the marsh is the cause of the bad climate that causes the death of so many men of Famagusta, exacerbated by their excessive enjoyment of women.

Where Saint Catherine was born

As Our Lord Jesus Christ allowed me to see the actual locations of all that happened to Saint Catherine - her prison in Alexandria and the glorious martyrdom she suffered in honour of our Lord Jesus

Christ on a wheel between two pillars, which I have already described in full, as well as the great mountain where her glorious body was carried by the holy angels and the monastery, where her precious body was later taken - I wanted to see where she was born. And so, on 5 December, I went to ancient Constantia, four miles from Famagusta. It was a sizeable city, built by the emperor Constus, the father of Saint Catherine, but now it is completely destroyed. I found what seemed to be the site of the castle, apparently a sizeable building, in which was the exact room, now in ruins, where Saint Catherine was born. Nearby is a much venerated chapel, where people from Famagusta regularly go to worship.

The great cistern

In the centre of where the castle used to be is an ancient cistern, which I think must be the biggest in the world. It has a vault supported by thirty-six pillars, with vents above for the water to flow in from the mountain. It ran all through the year on an aqueduct, like the one near Scauri on the territory of the castle of Traetto or Garigliano.

Where Saint Catherine was betrothed as a bride of Christ by an angel

In Famagusta I was told a story about Saint Catherine, that I cannot remember for the moment if it is included in her Life. As she grew up to be the most beautiful and clever of all women, her father and mother wanted to find her a husband. Saint Catherine, possessed by divine love, said: "I do not wish to take a husband unless he is as handsome, clever and rich as me." Her mother the empress, seeing that her daughter's mind was made up, said:

"My daughter, you are asking for something I cannot help you with, a man who is as handsome, clever and rich as you. On an island not far from here lives a hermit who serves God. Go and ask him if he knows of any man as endowed with as much nobility, beauty and wisdom as you." Saint Catherine replied: "I am prepared to do this," and went to find the hermit. When she asked his advice on the choice of a husband he said: "I cannot recommend any man to be your husband, with the exception of one, who is as clever, wise, handsome and rich as you." Saint Catherine said: "Who are you talking about?" The hermit replied: "Our Lord Jesus Christ." Then Saint Catherine said: "I wish him to be my husband and Lord and only him will I serve." While she spent the night there, an angel of the Lord came down from heaven and betrothed her with a ring on behalf of Our Lord Jesus Christ and received her as bride of Christ.

And so on 6 December I went to the island where Saint Catherine was betrothed by the angel as a bride of Christ. It is two bowshots from Famagusta near the port and is about an acre in size. It has a much venerated church of Saint Catherine.

Leaving Famagusta for Nicosia

Wishing to visit the Holy Cross of Cyprus, on which the good thief was crucified, I left at dawn on Wednesday 9 December for Nicosia, where the King of Cyprus lives. For a reasonable price I rented a cart to take me. The owner, who was Greek, sat me down next to him and had me drive the oxen. He got upset with me several times because I drove poorly and used the whip too much. I did not know what to do, as I had never done it before. After putting up with his criticism all day, we came to a farmhouse, where I slept on a mat on the floor. In those parts there are no beds to be had, even for ready money, and virtually everyone sleeps on the floor. The island is so overrun with fleas that it is impossible to sleep at night as they keep pigs inside the house. I got up early and, giving up the cart, continued my journey to Nicosia on foot. I had no wish to put up with any more criticism from the carter, who never stopped criticising me for whipping his oxen and driving his cart badly.

Nicosia

On Thursday 10 December I walked all day and arrived in Nicosia as the sun went down. As far as I could tell the city is about the size of Aversa. Down the middle of the city runs a little stream that you cross on stepping stones when it is not raining. When it does rain, there is a lot of water, so there are several stone or wooden bridges for people to cross. In some parts of town there are not many inhabitants but several fine houses. The palace of the King of Cyprus is rather beautiful. It has a courtyard as big as that of the Castel Nuovo in Naples and many fine buildings around it. Among them is a large hall, at the head of which is a fine throne with many beautiful pillars and ornamentation. I think there are few thrones like it, if any. Around the room runs a gallery with decorated columns. I was bold enough to go up to the entrance of the King's apartment and, if the door had been open, I would have gone in and discussed matters with him. In the courtyard is a well with good water, which many townspeople fetch for their own use.

The King lives most of the time in Nicosia after he lost Famagusta. He loves hunting and has twenty-four leopards and three hundred hawks of all kinds, and takes some out to hunt every day.

Saint Sophia

Nicosia has an archbishop and the cathedral is dedicated to Saint Sophia. It is a beautiful building with a vaulted nave painted blue with gold stars from the choir to the high altar. The annual income of the cathedral used to be twenty-five thousand ducats but the King of Cyprus has appropriated many of its entitlements.

The monasteries and the state of the town

In Nicosia there are some very fine monasteries and holy places, like Saint Francis, Saint Dominic, Saint Augustine. All the monasteries have two cloisters, one large and one small, with orange trees and other fruits. In the town are many gardens and orchards and fields planted with forage, wheat and barley. Indeed I saw next to the monastery of Saint Augustine, inside the city walls, a field planted with wheat and barley. And I saw the gardens of Saint Theodore, also inside the walls, planted with cabbages and various other vegetables. It all looks like Alife with its orchards and gardens inside the town. They have plenty of bread and wine. The wine is generally pleasant and stored in jars as they do not have casks. I would have liked to stay there for a month or so, as bread and wine were plentiful, but could not because there are no hotels with beds for foreigners. Had a good woman called Ambrosa, who was from the West, not found me a room with a bed, for the love of God, I would have had to sleep on the floor while I was there.

The Holy Cross of Cyprus

I wanted to see the Holy Cross of the Good Thief, called the Cross of Cyprus. After the morning meal on 15 December I left Nicosia and took the road without a guide to the mountain of the Holy Cross. I walked all day and in the evening, very tired and apprehensive, I came to a farmhouse that was still a day's walk from the church of the Holy Cross. I hoped to pay for a bed for the night to rest and gather strength but could only get a mat on the floor. I slept very badly because I was bitten alive all night by the accursed fleas. So I got up very early, hired a donkey, and in the intense cold came to a farmhouse on the lower slopes of the Holy Cross mountain. I bought something to eat and set off up the mountain. It was eight miles to the top and was in fact several mountains one after the other. They are all covered in trees they call *zibini,* mountain pines, which produce a lot of cones without any seeds. They grow abundantly, and provide roof shingles and firewood. With how much foreboding, toil and sweat, weakness of heart and body, I climbed those mountains to the church, God only knows! I got there by evening. The church is small but much venerated. On the right is a small chapel, in which the cross hovers in mid air without being attached to anything, a wonderful miracle. In the cross is a small piece of the wood of the cross of Our Lord Jesus Christ, in a silver case. After I had seen, examined and adored the cross, the monks who lived there showed me the following relics:

A long bone of Saint Agnes

An arm of Saint Blaise

A nail hammered into the hand of Christ

A rib of Saint George

A stone used to stone Saint Stephen
And a piece of the cross

Leaving the Cross of Cyprus

After I had reverenced the relics, I asked the
monks, as the abbot was away, if they would let me
sleep there that night. I said I was very tired and it
was a long and arduous way back and I was not sure
that I could find my way down to the farm where I
started from that morning. Such was their
ungodliness that they refused to let me stay the night,
saying that the abbot kept the keys to the rooms. And
so, in low spirits, I set off. I was more exhausted by
the way down than the way up. By the will of God,
my comfort, I kept going with frequent drinks of
water from the many streams flowing down the Holy
Mountain and at sunset arrived back at the
farmhouse, so exhausted that I thought my spirit
would take leave of my body. There I met the abbot
of the monastery, which owned the farm. I
complained vociferously to him about the mean-
spiritedness of his brothers in refusing to put me up.
The abbot was not pleased with this and took me to
his house. For the love of God he gave me bread and
wine and a mat to sleep on that night and wood for
the fire because of the extreme cold. And so I spent
the night there.

Leaving the farm

At dawn on 16 December I took leave of the
abbot and set off for Famagusta. I walked with a poor
pilgrim from Saint Elijah of the Benedictine abbey of
Monte Casino, whom I befriended as a brother
pilgrim. We walked all day in the pouring rain until in
the evening we came to the farm where I could not

get a bed at any price. A good Greek farmer let me sleep on the straw in a corner of the stable where he kept his oxen and asses. It was the best of beds.

Back in Famagusta

On the morning of 18 December I got up early and set off for Famagusta. I went past pans producing quantities of salt, and came to the castle of Baffa in the territory of the King of Cyprus that produces quantities of sugar. Walking all day I came across many farms destroyed by the Turks and abandoned. In the evening I came to a tavern by the side of the road run by a poor woman with five boys, two of whom were in diapers. I offered her money to make up a bed for me where I could rest my weary limbs. She made me a little bed next to the fire where she slept with her two babies and told me to go and sleep next to them. Seeing that the bed was not big enough for me and it was filthy from the babies, I refused to sleep there and spent the night on the floor, very cross. I got up in the morning and continued on my way to Famagusta. I arrived there on 28 December.

VIII

FROM CYPRUS TO RHODES

Leaving Famagusta

There was nothing in the world I wanted more than to get home. I found a Genoese pinnace in the port of Famagusta that was due to sail to Rhodes with pilgrims from Galicia and Hungary. I gave the captain two ducats to take me to Rhodes where I hoped to find Sir Antonatio and take passage with him back home. And so, on the morning of Thursday 7 January, I left Famagusta on the pinnace. We crossed the Gulf of Antalya, which is susceptible to storms at any time of year but we had good weather, thanks be to God.

Kastellorizo (Castro Ruczo)

On Sunday evening we arrived at Kastellorizo, which is held by the Order of Saint John of Jerusalem of Rhodes. The castle is built on a mountain and there are two hundred households. It is a mile across the sea to the mountains of Turkey.

Where Nicholas of Bari was born

Nearby on the Turkish coast is a ruined castle called Myra (*Ssammira*), where Saint Nicholas of Bari in Apulia was born. The people of Kastellorizo have many vineyards on the mainland. They went across to cultivate them as there was a truce with the Turks at that time.

Unable to enter the port of Rhodes.

On Monday night we did not enter the port of Rhodes, although we were only a mile away, because our captain was afraid of pirates. In the morning we could not get in because the wind was against us and also because the captain suspected that the pinnace of Martino Vincenzio, the Catalan pirate, was in port. Our captain turned away from Rhodes and headed to the island of Kos, wishing to get to Greece. Ah, God, how cross and depressed I was to be going away from the city where I hoped to find Sir Antonatio, for I had run out of money! It was the will of God, who always comes to the aid of the unfortunate, who hope in Him, that we were not far from Kos when an empty boat from Symi came towards us. It took me on board along with some German pilgrims, who were also on the pinnace from Famagusta, and undertook to take us to Rhodes for a ducat each. It took us to the island of Nisyros, which I described earlier. That night we slept on the beach in the terrible cold. The castle is more fortified than one can describe and the wine is excellent.

Symi (Ssimie)

On Wednesday morning we left Nisyros for Rhodes in great fear of Turkish ships sailing between the islands, as we were not able to get into the port that day. Late in the evening we sailed to Symi, which belongs to Rhodes and is about sixty miles in circumference. It was too late to land so we spent the night in great fear and cold in the lee of a cave by the shore. Symi has the best wine of all the islands. Jars of it are shipped every day for sale in Rhodes.

Rhodes

On the evening of Thursday 24 January we were overjoyed to land in Rhodes. I immediately found Sir Antonatio at the house of the Reverend Father in Christ, Fra' Dominic de Alemania, Preceptor of Naples and a fount of kindness. Fra' Dominic was informed of my situation by Sir Antonatio and, thanks to him, put me up in his house and entertained me at his table day and night for the whole month I was in Rhodes. He gave me a bed in his own room along with Sir Antonatio. Fra' Dominic extends many kindnesses to all foreigners coming to Rhodes, pilgrims and others. He always gives money to the needy and charity to the poor.

Works of charity of Saint John's hospital.

The works of charity of Saint John's Hospital, or rather the priors, are as follows. On three days every week they serve dinner to fourteen poor people in the great hall with the knights and other brothers. Each of them is served meat and four loaves and they take what is left over for their evening meal. No-one is ever left with less than half of the food given to them. On three other days of the week they distribute bread to all pilgrims and poor people who come to the hospital, one loaf each, about a hundred thousand in total. Many of the poor of both sexes lend their children to each other to carry and so get more free bread. This happens all through the year.

The ironwork of Tilos (Piscopia)

Fifty miles from Rhodes is the island of Tilos, whose inhabitants have the good fortune, by the grace and blessing bestowed by Saint Nicholas, that all their iron tools of whatever kind, never rust or get worn.

They prize their tools highly and make valuable gifts of them. I was reliably informed of this by Fra' Dominic and several other people. While I was in Rhodes I saw the following relics several times in the company of Fra' Dominic and other pilgrims.

Relics of Saint John

In the church of Saint John:
- an arm of Saint Stephen
- an arm of Saint George
- an arm of Saint Leo
- an arm of Saint Blaise
- a hand of Saint Clare
- the head of Saint Euphemia
- one of the thorns from Christ's crown
- a hand of Saint Agnes
- a cross containing hair of Our Lady and Saint Agnes
- money for the betrayal of Our Lord Jesus Christ

Relics of Saint John

In a beautiful chapel of Saint John
- an arm of Saint Catherine
- bones of Saint Theodore
- bones of Saint Titus and several other saints encased in a beautiful icon
- a thorn of the crown of Our Lord Jesus Christ at the moment of his glorious passion. I have it on good authority from several witnesses - so you should believe it - that every year on Good Friday at the hour when, for our salvation, Our Lord Jesus Christ was nailed to the cross and gave up his spirit, this thorn flowers and turns green and

comes into leaf in full view of everyone. It stays like this with flowers and leaves for half an hour.

- A silk and gold tapestry, woven by Saint Helena in memory and honour of the passion of Our Lord Jesus Christ, depicting Our Lord on the cross surrounded by angels.

Relics of Saint Catherine

Fra' Dominic de Alemania commissioned the building of the church of Saint Catherine inside the city. It has an excellent hostel with many rooms and good beds, which welcome all the pilgrims going to Jerusalem and other holy places overseas, including the nobility, since Rhodes lacks enough inns for pilgrims. I saw the following relics in the church.

- a piece of the sponge used to give Our Lord Jesus Christ bitter gall and vinegar to drink as he hung on the cross and said: "I am thirsty."
- a piece of the stick to which the sponge was fixed.
- a piece of the holy purple robe of Our Lord Jesus Christ
- a piece of the pink robe of Our Lady his mother
- a piece of another purple robe of Our Lord Jesus Christ
- a piece of the incorruptible coat of Our Lord Jesus Christ *
- a fragment of the cross of our Lord *
- a piece of John the Baptist's finger *
- a piece of bone of Saint Christopher *
- a piece of bone of Saint Theodore *
- a piece of bone of Saint Anastasia *
* These relics are enclosed in a large jasper case.

In Saint Catherinc's church are many venerated and beautiful icons containing twenty-five relics, all of whose labels I could not read. Those I could are as follows.

- a piece of bone of Saint Thomas
- a piece of bone of Saint Prosper
- a piece of bone of Saint Helena
- a piece of bone of Saint Theodore
- hair of Saint Agnes
- a piece of the veil of Our Blessed Lady
- a piece of bone of Saint Marcellinus

Fra' Dominic said that he was given all these relics by the emperor in Constantinople, who is his dear and lasting friend. They come from churches, which are reputed to have many beautiful relics and bodies of saints, men and women, from the time of the emperor Constantine, who built the city to look like Rome.

IX

THE CYCLADIC ISLANDS

Leaving Rhodes

On Monday 1 February we left Rhodes with many noble pilgrims from France coming from Saint Catherine's monastery on Sinai. We boarded a ship from Messina called Zono della Muta, paying five ducats a head to go to Venice. Sir Antonatio and I had a little cabin on the poop deck, just big enough for two, for which we paid a supplement of four ducats. In the cabin we stowed a good supply of wine, hardtack and several other things given to us by Fra' Dominic, which would have easily lasted us and our two servants until Venice, were it not for the misfortune that happened to us and that I will talk about later.

Kos

On Tuesday 2 February, forced off our direct course round the headland of Nisyros by a head wind, we headed for Kos and arrived in the harbour in the early evening. Sir Antonatio and I immediately went onshore in a little boat going to fetch water as we wanted to see the island and also the house of the very learned philosopher and doctor Hippocrates, who was from Kos. The town is on the sea and I guess about the size of Carinola, but the houses are in poor condition. The governor lives in the castle. He is a Knight of Saint John. The castle is between the sea and a lake that is about a third as big as the lake of Carinola. Water flows from the sea into the lake under the bridge of the castle so it is completely cut off and difficult to break into.

The house of Hippocrates

The house of Hippocrates is about twice a stone's throw outside the town. I think it used to be inside because the town was larger then. First we came to a fountain next to the house, with excellent water, which Hippocrates built and is now called the Fons Hippocratus. It seems the house was a large complex like a castle with many buildings. Now they are in ruins and some of them have been turned into stables.

The daughter of Hippocrates turned into a serpent and what happened to the monk who promised to kiss her.

Among the buildings is a big, deep cave. While I was in Rhodes, Fra' Dominic told me a remarkable story about it that he assured me was true. He said that the daughter of Hippocrates had changed into a serpent and lives in this cave. She often comes out and appears to people as a beautiful woman. She always asks for a man to kiss her while she is in the shape of a serpent, in return for which she promises many treasures and great riches and says she will take him as her husband. One day, not long ago, a Knight of Saint John came to live on Kos. It is the custom that every Knight who goes to Rhodes has to live for a year on Kos to help defend it, as it is near Turkey, or find someone to serve in his place. This Knight heard how the serpent came out of its cave and he went to see it while it was in the shape of a beautiful woman. The woman told him that if he agreed to kiss her as a serpent, she would give him many treasures and great riches. The Knight said he would and the woman said to him: "Look, I will show you how I will appear to you. Decide if you have the courage to come tomorrow and kiss me on the mouth and if not, tell me." He told her to show herself in whatever shape she turned into. The woman did this. She turned herself into a gigantic, vile, horrible serpent and then back into a woman. She asked the Knight what he was going to do. He replied that he was ready to do it and that he would come back the next day. The following morning the Knight got ready and mounted his horse and returned to the woman, who was now in the shape of a big, horrible serpent. Fearfully, he got down from his horse and went to kiss it. The serpent grew more terrible and vile. The terrified Knight jumped on his horse and fled. The serpent chased after him with a great roar as far as the castle, where the Knight escaped with his life. He lived for three days until he died of fright. They say on Kos that from time to time the serpent can still be seen outside the cave.

The island is one hundred and fifty miles around and is very rich in crops and animals. It brings an annual income to the governor of ten thousand ducats a year.

Leaving Kos

On Wednesday night we left the port of Kos. That day we passed several of the islands of the Archipelago, of which two were inhabited, one called Kalymnos (*Lu Calamo*) and the other Leros (*Lu Erro*), that were under the jurisdiction of Kos.

Naxos and Paros (Nicosia et Paris)

On Thursday we sailed past several islands, whose names I do not know, and about noon came to the island of Naxos, the seat of the Duke of the Archipelago. Many of the islands' rulers are subject to him and all are under the rule of Venice. That day we came to Paros. It has a large population. It is said that it gets its name from Paris, the son of Priam King of Troy, who was cast away here to be brought up by shepherds, because when he was born it was prophesied that Troy would be destroyed because of him. On Friday we passed many islands, two of which were inhabited, one called Siphnos *(Ciphanu)* and the other Kythnos *(Fermia)*, fifteen miles apart. They are under the jurisdiction of the Duke of the Archipelago.

The pirate ship that discovered us in the harbour and what happened next.

On the same day, Friday, in the late afternoon, our helmsman brought us into the harbour of Kythnos, unfortunately for us, as will become evident. We stayed several days because of contrary winds. While we there, a pirate ship came in belonging to Francisco del Casi, a Catalan. A head wind prevented him from coming near and he moored in another harbour not far from us, separated by a sandy beach. Three soldiers among us pilgrims went to their ship to ask about their intentions towards us. They replied with fine words and promises, saying that they intended no harm. For three days they repeated this promise while they waited for the wind to change so they could capture us. Eventually, one evening they deployed thirty crossbowmen on the shore to watch the beach so that no-one could escape from our boat to the town of Kythnos, in the hills eight miles from the harbour. They seized two of our sailors, who went to the town for help and were returning to the ship.

Seeing what happened and realising they wanted to take us, we had serious misgivings.

We escape from the ship

With threats and persuasion Sir Antonatio worked on our ship's captain to give us a small boat. We got on board with the minimum of baggage in the evening as the moon rose. Along with the captain, helmsman, bosun, paymaster and other sailors we set off very nervously as the little boat was so overloaded it threatened to sink at any moment. We came to a harbour a fair way from them, picked up our bags and abandoned the boat. We fled into the hills in fear on circuitous, difficult, and rocky paths, constantly stumbling and falling. I was carrying a bundle of belongings and clothes, mine and Sir Antonatio's, that weighed as much as a sack of grain. All that night we fled through the mountains in search of Kythnos town and safety while they came after us. O God! How frightened and sweating and trembling I was, with that heavy load on my back! I wondered in amazement where such a puny body, unused to such heavy toil, found so much strength. I concluded it was thanks to God and not my own doing.

Kythnos

At about mid-morning we arrived at Kythnos town, solidly built on a rock, which is all I can say about it. It is governed by Giovanni da Bologna. Not long before we arrived he had gone from Kythnos in a galley to the Duke of the Archipelago in Naxos. Along with Sir Simon de Mediolano, who escaped from the boat with us, we were given a room with two beds, where we stayed while we were on Kythnos. The governor's uncle, his son and several other good men looked after us very well for those days. After they looted it, the pirates gave our captain back his ship and the other pilgrims went back on board, having agreed with him to take them to Methoni for four hundred ducats. God help them because they put themselves in great danger.

Leaving Kythnos and our lenten meal on the beach

Continually thinking of how to get back home, we decided to go via Athens, which Venice had recently taken into its empire after the death of Duke Ranieri of Florence, whose dukedom it belonged to. Then we planned to go through the Morea to Corinth and from there, with the help of the Duke of Cephalonia, who was a friend of Sir Antonatio, to Venice or somewhere else on the way home. So we found a little boat to take us for ten ducats to Athens, eighty miles from Kythnos.

On 22 February, Shrove Monday, we had our morning meal in Kythnos and went down to the port where our boat was waiting. In the evening we had a carnival meal on the shore of little fish and various other things we brought with us. As soon as we had eaten we boarded the boat and in the middle of the night headed for Kea *(Cie)*, which belongs to Giovanni da Bologna. We slept a while in the harbour and then set off again at night, very afraid of Turkish vessels. We made for the port of Athens, five miles from the city, but could not go in because of contrary winds. So we went to another port twenty-three miles from Athens and disembarked in the evening of Shrove Tuesday 23 of February.

The man and woman changed into marble statues

On a hill not far from the port are two marble statues of a man and a woman. It is said that he used to be a real man who pursued the woman in order to take her virginity. She fled into the hills, refusing to let him have his way. Seeing she could not escape him, she begged God to turn both of them into marble statues. Her prayer was heard and so they remain to this day.

X

ATHENS CHALCIS CORINTH

Lenten meal on Tuesday in the port of Athens (Acthena)

On Shrove Tuesday we kept the vigil of Saint Matthew the Apostle, according to my calendar, and had our carnival meal on the beach. We had bread, cheese, and egg and cheese pies given to us in Kythnos. With what sighs, with what despair in heart and soul, did I eat that meal, thinking I was in permanent exile without any hope of a vessel to take me home. I thought of the despair of my household and all my relatives and friends to whom I could send no news of my plight. I thought of carnival meals at home with so many different dishes, plenty not only for my household but also for the needy and poor of the neighbourhood. Over those days the drops of wine I drank were fewer than the tears that flowed from my eyes, constantly giving due praise to God, so that he would let me complete my journey and save me from the clutches of pirates.

Leaving the port

Far from home and in fear of the Turks who roamed around the area we hired for a ducat two pack animals and a horse from some local fishermen to take us to the city of Athens, twenty-four miles away. We set off at dusk and walked the whole night in the rain across hills and lonely valleys until we arrived in Athens on the morning of Wednesday 24 February.

Athens

From the evidence of ancient buildings and the works of scholars and writers, Athens was a great city with great buildings, as we saw from the many columns and marble blocks lying around where the city used to be. It stretched as far as the sea and was twenty-four miles in circumference at the time of the Emperor Hadrian, who ruled it. Then it was destroyed by the Trojans and reduced to the area around the castle. The city lies between two hills six miles apart on a fine plain twelve miles long with many good olive groves. Now the city has about a thousand households.

Fountains where students used to drink

I wanted to visit the antiquities of the city and asked some locals to be my guide. First we went to two fountains where students had to drink the water to acquire knowledge. By this the writers meant that the source of knowledge from which they should drink was the study of the great philosophers like Aristotle and others who lived in the city. Both fountains were beautifully worked and sculpted in marble. We then went to Aristotle's school. *(The Lyceum?)* It is built of marble, twenty feet long and sixteen feet wide. It was roofed with marble architraves and entablatures above them. The whole building around and overhead was decorated with various reliefs in gold and other beautiful colours. Traces of decoration can be seen at both ends of the room. Outside the door are porticos with columns supporting marble architraves and entablatures, sculpted and painted in gold, where Aristotle used to stroll to relax when he was tired of studying. We then went to where Hadrian's palace once stood, now in ruins *(Temple of Olympian Zeus)*. Twenty columns survive, eighty feet tall and wide enough for four men together to put their arms round. Long, thick marble architraves span the columns to support what was a great building.

Entrance to the castle

Nearby is what used to be the entrance gate to the castle *(The Arch of Hadrian?)*. It is made of marble, beautifully carved, as beautiful as the entrance to the tower of Capua but not as tall in my opinion. Outside the city is a great bridge with a large barracks. Soldiers used to run out from both sides and do battle in the middle *(Olympic Stadium)*

The castle and its great hall

We then went up to the castle, which is built on a marble outcrop. Inside is a great hall with thirteen tall columns *(Propylaea?)*. On top of the columns are thirty foot long marble architraves and entablatures. It is a beautiful sight.

The great church of Athens and its beautiful buildings

Then we went into the great church inside the castle, dedicated to Saint Mary. *(Parthenon)* It is built of big marble blocks joined with lead and is as large as the church in Capua. Around the church on the outside are sixty great columns. Each is higher than ladders used for the harvest and wide enough for five men together to put their arms round. Long, thick architraves sit on top of the columns and support the portico of the church. The human mind cannot imagine how they could construct such a large building.

The column marked by Saint Dionysius

One of these columns bears a sign. It is the one Saint Dionysius was chained to at the time of the passion of Our Lord Jesus Christ. When all the buildings in the world began to shake in the earthquake Saint Dionysius proclaimed: "Either the world is coming to an end or the Son of God will suffer," and traced the sign of the cross on the column with his fingers. The cross is still to be seen on the column.

As far as I could gauge, the entrance to the church is twenty five feet wide and thirty feet high. The doors belonged to the city of Troy. When it was destroyed, they were brought to Athens and became the doors of Saint Mary's church.

The first altar

The church has two naves, one after the other. In the first is the first altar in the world, made by Saint Dionysius after his conversion to the Catholic faith.

Jasper columns

The choir of the church is impressive. Around the altar are four columns made of jasper, wide enough for two men to join hands around and twelve feet high. On top of these columns is a fine baldaquin over the high altar. Nearby is a large cistern into which quantities of water pour when it rains.

The icon of the Virgin Mary painted by Saint Luke

In a little chapel nearby, to the right of the altar, is a painting of Our Lady the Virgin Mary by Saint Luke the Evangelist. It is decorated with pearls, gems and many other precious stones and closely guarded under lock and key. Around the church are eighty marble columns supporting long marble architraves and entablatures above which a frieze runs all round the church. In a crack in the wall a light glows that never goes out. It is thought that the body of a saint is buried inside.

The relics

On that day the custodians of the church showed us the following holy relics.

The head of Saint Macarius of Jerusalem.

An arm bone of Saint Denis of France.

An arm of Saint Cyprian.

An arm of Saint Justina

A bone of the Holy Maccabees.

A book of all the gospels in Saint Helena's hand on gold illuminated parchment in Greek, considered a priceless treasure.

A statue

Outside the walls of the castle are two great columns said to have supported a marvellous shrine containing a statue so powerful that, in those days, if enemy vessels approached, however far out to sea they appeared, the statue sank them. But if they were well-intentioned the statue did them no harm *(Athena Promachos)*.

Leaving Athens

We could not travel overland to Corinth because of a serious dispute between the Duke of Cephalonia and the Despot of Morea, a brother of the Emperor of Constantinople, about the hereditary lands of Lord Ranieri, Duke of Athens, who was father-in-law to both the Duke and the Despot. The Duke had a large army of Turks with him, having made an alliance with the Turkish Sultan against the Despot. And so we set off on Friday 25 February to the island of Evia *(Nigropont)*, which belongs to the Venetians, in the hope of finding a ship to Venice. We rode the whole day on donkeys because we could not find any horses for hire in Athens. Late in the evening, after nightfall, we arrived at the castle of Sykamino *(Zucchamino)*, occupied by the Knights of Saint John of Jerusalem.

Turkish threat

On that day Turkish cavalry scoured the land around the castle, capturing people and animals. In the afternoon, as luck would have it, we went down a road that the Turks had been down about an hour earlier. God willed that the man in Athens who had hired us donkeys palmed us off with inferior animals, which is why we took longer than we should, because otherwise we would have fallen into their hands. Often the proverbs are true that say many setbacks can sometimes turn out for the best.

Sykamino castle

While we were in the moat near the lower slope of the castle, some of the knights, on the alert after the Turkish forays and who had seen us from a distance, charged down at us and we were afraid they were Turks. That evening we reached the castle where the governor graciously received us out of respect for Fra' Dominic de Alemania, of whom he knew Sir Antonatio to be a very dear friend.

Chalcis (Nigropont)

On the morning of the following Friday, 26 February, the governor lent us horses to go down to the sea three miles from Sykamino and gave us an escort. We boarded a little fishing boat that took us to Chalcis. We were graciously received by noblemen of the city, partners in a newly built inn. We were given a fine room with two excellent beds for Sir Antonatio, Sir Simon and me and other beds for our servants. O God! How potent and benevolent in God's eyes is the kindness of hospitality, for Our Lord Jesus Christ himself often obtained lodging with Saint Julian in the shape of his precious followers.

Chalcis

The island of Evia is three hundred miles in circumference and is separated from the mainland, the Dukedom of Athens, by a channel twelve yards wide or so. The city of Chalcis is situated beside the channel at one end of the island. It is smaller than the city of Sessa but heavily populated with Latins and Greeks. The island has several castles and villages with fourteen thousand families in all. The main church is beautiful and dedicated to Saint Mary. In former times the city was three times the size but destroyed in war. Now it is reduced to a site next to the channel. Outside the city are dwellings and ancient buildings. They include the large and handsome church of Saint Francis where the friars live from their own resources. A custodian told me that the church has now an annual income of about a thousand ducats. Not far from the church is a convent of nuns dedicated to Saint Clara.

The ancient castle

In the middle of the channel that separates the island from the mainland is an ancient and tall building said to be the castle of Morgan le Fay, Lady of the Lake, the mother of Pulzella Gaia, the Merry Maid. Sir Gawain is supposed to have been held captive there. *(Jealous of her dragon-daughter's fling with Gawain, Morgan imprisons him in a bewitched castle to have her way with him.)*

The bridges

Two wooden bridges cross the channel on either side of the castle. People going from the mainland to the island pass over them and through the castle. The bridges and the gates are closely guarded by armed sentries. There are two ports. The water flows like a river from one port to the other, sometimes one way and then the other.

The mills

There are three mills in the channel, ingeniously constructed so that they grind grain whichever direction the water flows. Each of them brings in fifty ducats a year. Sometimes the current is so strong that the mill-wheels break. The city is surrounded by the sea on three sides and has fine walls and many towers all around. It boasts rich and noble men and beautiful women. I think all the women have inherited from the fairies who lived in the castle their good looks and lovely clothes, in the Italian fashion.

We waited six weeks for the ship to arrive from Venice, our hearts and minds full of anxiety and without any news of its arrival. And so, having taken the advice of the Governor of Evia and armed with letters of recommendation from him, we decided to go back to Athens and from there find transport back home.

Leaving Chalcis

After the morning meal on Friday 2 April we left Chalcis on a little boat and arrived at sunset in the port of Sykamino, eighteen miles away. We disembarked and went up on foot to the castle, three miles from the sea. We were very nervous as the castle is close to another called Oropos *(Ripos)*, manned by Albanians, who were robbers and committed all sorts of crime whenever they could.

Leaving Sykamino by night

We got to the castle and had something to eat. At dusk we left again. We walked all night with fear and fatigue across rugged, rocky mountains and valleys, on rough and tortuous tracks, constantly afraid from one valley to the next of meeting Albanians or Turks who were in the habit of lying in wait for plunder in these parts. We walked all night in fear and fatigue and great danger but with the help of God arrived without incident .

Athens

In the middle of the afternoon on the Saturday before Palm Sunday we arrived in Athens, hoping to find my Lord Luigi di Prata, archbishop of the city, but he was in Corinth with the Duke of Cephalonia. We met with the bishop his deputy and some of his household, whom he had sent to take possession of and administer the property of his church. We had no alternative but to stay with them that night as we could not find an inn.

Leaving Athens

On Palm Sunday 4 April we heard mass and received palms in the little and impoverished church of Saint Dominic, where there are only two friars. We left Athens with pack animals that we hired to take us to the castle of Megara, which the Duke of Cephalonia had recently taken over for his wife, the daughter of Duke Ranieri. It is twenty-three miles from Athens. We walked on foot or on horseback the whole day in fear of brigands and Turks ever on the lookout for loot. In the late afternoon, fifteen miles from Athens, we came to the castle of Eleusis *(Lippissinox)*. It used to be a great and distinguished city, as was obvious from the ruined buildings and columns. Water came into the city from the mountains on aqueducts with pillars and arches. When it was still intact the city was ten miles in circumference.

Megara castle (Metre)

About two hours after sunset we reached Megara. We were not allowed in as it was zealously guarded for fear of the Despot of Morea, who claimed it from the Duke, his brother-in-law, for his wife, who was also a daughter of Lord Ranieri. And so we spent the night in a little church outside the walls beside the moat. Still fearful, we kept watch all night.

Leaving Megara

Megara is in fertile plain and has eighty homes. On the morning of Monday 5 April we found a small boat hardly big enough to take the five of us. We paid five bezants to go to Corinth and left after the morning meal. We rowed the whole day and at dusk arrived at the port of Corinth, fifteen miles from the city. In the port were two other boats from Megara, whose sailors told us that we would not be able to get into Corinth *(Acrocorinth, the acropolis of ancient Corinth)* without risk to our lives at the hands of the Despot's men. He had recently laid siege to Corinth with a great army of about twenty thousand, claiming the city for his wife, the elder daughter of Lord Ranieri. The Duke, seeing that he could not resist the might of his brother-in-law, made an alliance with the Turks against the Despot. And so one night about forty thousand Turkish cavalry headed for Corinth and made a surprise attack on the Despot's camp, destroying it along with the army and taking three thousand knights prisoner. The Despot himself barely managed to escape. But after the Turks left, the Despot's wife still had a large force that patrolled Corinthian territory day and night, so hardly anyone could get through without being captured.

Leaving the port for Corinth

Asking round the port, we found a man from Corinth who knew the hidden paths that would take us safely into Corinth. We paid him and two other sailors to come with us and show us the safe way up. We set out on foot with them on byways through arid ravines and hills, avoiding dangerous tracks and places in fear and silence, thinking we would come across the enemy at any moment. We walked the whole night with how much toil, fear and anxiety, only God knows - and we who endured this trial! In truth I thought several times that my spirit would leave my body but thanks be to God we came to the top of the mountainous rock and the city of Corinth. We arrived at the gates about midnight and slept outside for the rest of the night.

Corinth

The next morning, Tuesday 6 April, we entered the city of Corinth and paid our respects to the Duke. With him was the archbishop, who took us into his house, for there were neither inns to be found nor bread for sale. With the help of the archbishop, we obtained permission from the Duke to go on one of his brigantines that had come to Corinth to bring his wife back to his island of Cephalonia. That morning the sailors, who had brought us up and were going back to the port, were captured not far from the city, which showed the danger we had been in the night before.

Ancient Corinth

Many remarkable things are told in the West about Corinth, which are not true. But I shall tell the truth and clear up any misunderstanding. It is true that the city used to be great and famous in the time of King Alexander. Then it was in a different place, namely on the plain between the hill where it now stands and the port. From the evidence of ancient buildings it appears to have been a great and remarkable city, about ten miles in circumference. All the houses were roofed with lead and other types of metal. When it was besieged by the Romans, who then ruled the whole world, it caught fire and was completely burnt to the ground. As a result, the lead and other metal on the burning houses melted and flowed through the streets down to the port. And so the great and celebrated city was destroyed. It was the favourite of all King Alexander's cities and he would give it to no-one.

New Corinth

The city is now on top of a mountainous rock surrounded by rough-built walls. Sir Antonatio and I walked all the way round, which we reckoned was about two miles. The houses inside the walls are in poor condition and there are many open spaces. I think that in all the empty space you could not sow more than three bushels of grain. The city has about fifty homes. On a mound inside the city is an ugly-looking castle that is difficult to get into.

The port of Corinth

The city is near two ports, fifteen miles from one and four miles from the other, where the old city used to be. The distance between the ports is six miles. They are separated by a strip of land now called Examilia *(Sexmilia)*. King Alexander once wanted to dig a canal from one bay to another so that Corinth and the whole of the Peloponnese, which belonged to him, would become an island. He was not able to dig a canal because the ground is very rocky but you can still see the ditches from that time. Instead he had a massive high wall built from one port to the other so no-one could cross to attack Corinth. In some places the wall is still standing and in others it is in ruins. These were and are the true facts about Corinth.

It is also true that it has the best currants and raisins and good figs, of which we ate our fill with the Archbishop of Athens.

XI

FROM CORINTH TO ITALY

Leaving Corinth

On Wednesday 7 April the Duke, intending to send his wife the Duchess to his island of Cephalonia, ordered all his men, soldiers and civilians alike, to arm and prepare themselves to escort her to the port, for fear of the Despot's men.

The church of Saint Paul, where he was held prisoner

First we visited the little church of Saint Paul, where he was held prisoner while he wrote his letters to the Corinthians. He was chained to a pillar on which you can see the cross he scratched with his own finger. We went apprehensively down to the port with the Duke's men and the Duchess. She and her retinue boarded one brigantine and we another.

At sea

We headed towards Patras, a hundred miles from Corinth, down the gulf between the Despotates of the Morea and Arta. Its width varies between two and six miles.

Aigio (Posticza)

In the middle of the afternoon on Thursday 8 April, we came to a town called Aigio in the Despotate of Morea on the Peloponnese coast, a bowshot from the sea. It is prosperous, the size of Carinola and has a handsome castle belonging to the Despotate. It is now the possession of a man called

Burdus, who seized it along with some other towns of the Peloponnese, with his Navarrese army.

Tolofon (Vetranicze)

On the coast of the despotate of Albania, is a town called Tolofon, which is now held by the Grand Turk, the Sultan. It used to belong to his mother-in-law Dominica de Sola, who possessed several towns in the despotate. Because of the many provocations and injuries she endured from the Despot of Morea, she gave her only daughter in marriage to the Sultan, along with all her lands. The Sultan, who was an enemy of the despot, married her to get the land, which was next to that of despot, in order to raid his territory and do battle with him. We were told that the Sultan then did away with the wife because she was not worthy of him. This is how the Sultan acquired the territory and the reason why the Turks always go through it on the way to attack neighbouring territories.

Lepanto (Nepanto)

On the late afternoon of the same day we came to a fine castle called Lepanto, that belongs to the Despotate of Arta. At that moment a sudden squall blew up with such a rough sea that if our brigantine had not been decked over the waves would have swamped it. We ran before the storm and danger to the port of Patras, which we reached that day at sunset. The town itself is two bowshots from the sea.

Patras (Patrax)

At dusk we entered the town of Patras. We could not find anywhere to stay, neither an inn nor in the Franciscan friary of Saint Nicholas. But the archbishop of Patras, who was a friend of Sir Antonatio, welcomed us into his beautiful palace. It has a hall twenty-five feet long, whose walls are painted all round with scenes of the destruction of Troy. The archbishop is a Franciscan. The city and several other towns are subject to him in temporal and spiritual matters. In former days he received an annual income of twenty-five thousand ducats but now it is only fifteen thousand.

Leaving Patras

On Good Friday we found a ship from Corfu that had come into Patras. We agreed a fare of five ducats to take all five of us to Corfu. We went to the Good Friday service and paid visits to various churches, as is the custom on that day among Catholic Christians. Among them was the church of Saint Andrew, half a mile outside the city, which is the seat of the Archbishop and has a fine vaulted nave. We also went to another church, where the Apostle Andrew, who preached the faith of Christ in those parts, was arrested and imprisoned. At dusk we went down to the shore and, after a nap to gather our strength, boarded our boat and set off for Corfu.

The river that crosses the sea

On Holy Saturday we came to the island of Oxeia *(Coczolara)*. We had dinner on the ship because we were fasting before the Blessed Easter of the Resurrection of the Lord. In the late afternoon we crossed a bay into which flows the Achelous *(Cathoschi)* river. It flows so fast through the sea for twenty miles that its water does not mix with sea water. While we crossed it we took it up and drank it, marvellously sweet. The water stayed fresh for a bowshot across the bay.

The island of Lefkada (Lucate) and the castle of Santa Maura (Mafra).

In the mid-afternoon on Easter Sunday we reached the island of Lefkada, a hundred miles from Patras, on which there is a small castle by the name of Santa Maura belonging to the Duke of Cephalonia. It is three miles or more across the gulf to the mainland and the large province of Albania, ruled by the Despot of Arta. Lefkada was formerly joined to Albania by a narrow tongue of land. Then, because the Albanians used to make incursions, it was dug through so that now the castle is surrounded by water and the Albanians from the mainland can no longer cause trouble. Simon of Genoa and Ciccarello of Naples, governor of the castle, honoured Sir Antonatio with many gifts.

Leaving Santa Maura

At dawn on Monday we left the castle of Santa Maura and headed to Corfu, where we could find our passage home. A contrary wind caused us to put into a fairly good port on the Albanian coast. Around the port was a lovely forest of oak, laurel and other tall trees, home to many wild animals. We stayed in port three days because of the unfavourable winds. Every night in the harbour fish, big and small, made an incredible noise with their fighting and racketing and chasing each other so we could not sleep on the shore. I think it was a sign of the ill luck that befell us on our journey.

Leaving port

At dawn on Thursday 15 April we left that port. When we were four miles out to sea a south westerly wind came up and the sea got rougher. We had not gone far when the wind whipped up the waves against us, with peals of thunder and flashes of lightning and hail and torrential rain. We begged the captain to take us back to land, for it seemed dangerous to sail on in such a rough sea. He refused, saying that the storm would not last long and he wanted to get to a port ten miles away, where he trusted that we would be quite safe.

The great storm

The gale whipped up the sea and it looked as if our little boat would be plunged into the depths. The waves grew higher and higher and tossed the boat from the trough up to the crest and from the crest down to the trough. The crew realised we were in serious danger and wanted to head back to land but could not because of the violence of the storm. It grew worse and worse, the waves battered the boat and the sail and often came over the side. Stricken with fear we commended ourselves unceasingly to Almighty God, begging the captain and the crew to run us aground on land if they could and not to let us perish so cruelly. The captain and crew told us that they could do nothing to escape our mortal danger. They could not head for the shore because of sandbanks and reefs and they could not steer out to sea against the headwind. Seeing they were near to death, according to the Greek custom, they took out bread, blessed it and gave themselves communion. What did I, poor Nicholas the lawyer, and my companions think of but death? "Ah God! I said to myself, I hoped to die at home and for my body to be honourably buried in my robes in my chapel of Saint Catherine, where my parents and my sons are buried. But now I see I am to die a bitter and obscure death far from my country and my body, after my soul has left it, washed up on the shore by the waves to be eaten by wild animals. If only I had died on the high sea so its depths would be my grave! Who will announce my death to my wife so that she puts on black and leads the life of a widow? Who will tell the Archdeacon of Carinola, my brother, so he executes my will according to my wishes? Oh how bitter is the life of those who wait! They will wait for me, day after day, and no-one will come with definite news of the end of my life." Weeping bitter tears, all my senses were numbed. I was devoid of all courage. Even the light in my eyes was dimmed. I begged God to have mercy on my sins, to receive my soul that I commended to him, and to snatch it from the mouth of the lion and the net of the hunters.

Driven aground

Sir Antonatio, despite his fear of the sea, helped with the boat and encouraged the crew. As a result of his concern they turned the boat towards the shore. With the strength of the wind and the force of the waves behind us they succeeded in steering it to the shore through a narrow gap between two reefs, where we ran aground. A sailor immediately jumped out with a rope and made us fast. One after the other we disembarked safely holding on to the rope. Since I am not very tall it was harder for me to get out than for the others and I was up to my chest in the water. So, with the help of God and Our Lord Jesus Christ, who does not want the death of a sinner but that he should reform and live, we were all rescued from mortal danger.

Note

I want to say one thing to all those who read and hear about these dangers and trials, that they should not be frightened or put off if they are thinking about undertaking this holy and precious journey. They do not always happen to pilgrims and, when they do, are good for the soul. So it is said: "who does not work does not eat," and "he does not deserve sweetness who has not tasted bitterness."

Let us not cease to strive for our salvation in honour of Our Lord Jesus Christ, who chose to be crucified in Jerusalem for our salvation and suffered death with such agony and abuse.

Our boat was so battered by the waves on the shore that it broke up. Men from a castle belonging to the Despot of Arta, called Preveza, two miles from the coast, came and dragged it out of the water.

The castle

The governor of the castle, who was from Naples, took pity on us and sent a servant with a horse. We got to the castle in fear of Albanians in the vicinity. The governor let us sleep in a hay loft for three days until our ship was repaired.

Leaving the castle

As soon as the boat was repaired we left the castle of Preveza *(Arevesse)* on Monday 19 April. At sunset we docked in the port of the castle of Fanari, belonging to Venice.

Fanari Castle

The castle is on mound on a hill, making it three times as high as the great tower of Carinola castle and unassailable by anyone. We slept at the port until midnight, when we left and sailed six miles along the Albanian coast to the castle of Parga, belonging to the Despot of Arta.

Corfu (Gorfo)

In the middle of the afternoon on Tuesday 20 April we arrived at the port of Corfu. It is a fine island, a hundred and sixty miles around. It used to belong to the King of Naples and now belongs to Venice. The city is built on a corner of the island and to my mind the size of the city of Teano. But most of the houses are run-down and the streets are narrow. It is close to the sea and has two gates. There are two castles inside the city on tall mounds a bowshot from each other. From the outside they look strong and well guarded. The town outside the citadel has a large population, and is where the taverns and inns are found.

At dawn on Monday we left Corfu and at sunset arrived at the port of Sazan *(Casopoli)*, where there is a church dedicated to Saint Mary, a stone's throw from the sea. It has a much venerated icon of the Blessed Virgin Mary that produces miracles every day. It used to be a large town but was abandoned so they say, because of a plague of snakes. It is now completely ruined. There were many walls and several towers, which the Venetians demolished.

XII

THROUGH ITALY TO CARINOLA

We left Sazan at five in the morning of Thursday 6 May and arrived at the port of San Cataldo in the region of Apulia, a hundred and twenty miles from Corfu, where there is a fortress belonging to Sir Raymond de Nola. On the same day we sailed six miles from San Cataldo to Lecce *(Liccium)*. It is a big city, the size of Aversa, as far as we could tell. They say it has four thousand homes. It has fine walls with more than a hundred towers and a stone-walled moat all around, a large and beautiful castle and lovely gardens.

On Monday 10 May Sir Raymond de Nola sent horses and his steward to fetch us to the town where he lived, San Pietro Galatino, ten miles from Lecce. Like the gracious lord he is, he received us with great honour and did us the favour of giving us an armed escort and paying our expenses throughout all his lands. So on 13 May we left Lecce for Oria *(Hoyra)*. From there we travelled to Grottaglie, ruled by Sir Mala Carne de Grottaglie. On the next day we went to Palagiano *(Paleano)*, the next to Altamura. From there we were escorted to Minervino by fifty cavalry provided by Sir Raymond. From Minervino we went to Lavello, Rocchetta, Grottaminarda, and Flumeri. We left Flumeri late in the day with thirty horsemen and twenty-five foot soldiers of Sir Raymond and walked all night for fear of the Bretons in Apice. At dawn we came to Benevento. We left there with the Vice-Rector and an escort of soldiers, passing through Appolosa *(Pollosa)* and Montesarchio to arrive at Arienzo *(Argentium)* in the evening. On Wednesday night we left apprehensively with twenty-five foot soldiers and reached Capua at dawn on Thursday, 27 May. We left Capua on the same day and as we reached Carinola many men of the town, out of kindness and their love for me, came out to Santa Croce to meet me. On the whole way into town it was amazing how many people came to welcome me. I do not say this out of empty self-glorification, for all self-praise is repellent, but to commend them for the love they showed me.

And so I came into town with them with immense joy, looking forward to the comfort of my dearest wife. I did not know that she had died at dawn on Holy Saturday 10 April, the hour of the resurrection of Our Lord Jesus Christ. Oh how bitter was that day! My wife Constantia, whom I loved above all for her goodness, was gone. She loved God more than anything, and her family and the poor of the neighbourhood. She often went to mass, always fasted twice a week, and gave alms to the poor on all the saints' vigils. She welcomed pilgrims into our home with the utmost charity, giving them food and a bed, not only those who came to the house but others she sent her servants to look for in the town. She arranged for the newborn babies of the poor to be baptised. She asked me to make a list of the names of all the children she had baptised. There were almost two hundred. Prayers or the Our Father were never far from her lips. So I hope that for all this and her great charity, her soul reigns with Christ.

When I got to my house and found my wife was not there, all spirit and sense were numbed by intense grief. I felt I could live no longer on this earth, all the more since I was sure she died from the immense grief I caused her by my belated return.

But considering that we are all born for this, as Boethius says: "It is the eternal and immutable law that nothing created endures," and that she was cared for in her illness by several doctors until she died, and that her body was placed with all due ceremony in my chapel on Holy Saturday, with a large number of mourners and my lord Bishop in all his vestments with his retinue, I give praise to Almighty God who called her to his kingdom with such a fine memorial.

This is the end of the story
Praise and Glory to Christ.
For the one who wrote this work
Let a place be kept in Paradise

This work was rewritten and copied at the La Rocca Spa of Mondragone by Ciccio Grosso di Balsorano on the instruction of Roger de Celano, who lives there, in March 1397 in the reign of his Serene Highness our Prince and Sovereign Ladislaus of Hungary, King of Jerusalem and Sicily etc.

Fourteenth Century St Catherine pilgrim badge

JOHN MOLE

POSTSCRIPT

A rare insight into a medieval mind.

Martoni did not know he had a medieval mind. He would have assumed he was 'modern', from the Latin 'modo', just now, at the culmination of the past and the cusp of the future. What is the difference between his modern mind and ours?

He negotiates his world in ways we would recognise, paying cash for food and shelter and transport. He is curious about it, describing noteworthy sights and sites and people he meets. His interaction with the physical world was similar to ours, except that he had less protection from it and little technology to deal with it. He confronts the sea in open boats, crosses the desert in summer on foot. Companions die in unforgiving conditions or from illness, for which there is no effective medicine. Wherever he travels, from Italy to Palestine, the constant threat from pirates, robbers, soldiers, can only be countered by travelling at night or across country or with an armed escort.

Martoni lived before the age of printing. His written sources of information are primarily the Latin Bible and legal documents. There are few other reliable texts. Maps are diagrammatic and will lead astray if used literally. He calls the Nile the Tigris because he confuses Babylon, the twin town of Cairo, with Babylon of the Bible. He tells us that Athens was built by the Emperor Hadrian and then destroyed by the Trojans. The Colossians to whom Saint Paul wrote were not inhabitants of Rhodes named after its Colossus but citizens of the town of Colossae in Asia Minor. Although he quotes them, there is no evidence that Martoni was familiar first hand with classical writers. He refers to the abduction of Helen by Paris and the fall of Troy but in distorted versions of the story. His acquaintance with the Iliad is is probably filtered through romances, anecdotes and tales acquired from performers, fabulists, marionette theatre and other forms of live entertainment. He does not mention the Odyssey, which is a pity, as his own journey home is a real-life version with several entertaining parallels.

While Martoni is generally well informed about the Bible, some of the stories he relates had long been expunged from canonical texts but remained alive in folklore and apocrypha. Saint Thomas was martyred in Chennai and his relics soon transferred to Edessa, whose diocese included the Malabar Coast of India. In neither place was his tomb surrounded by water. Indeed, by the time Martoni heard about them they had already been taken via Chios to Ortona in Italy, where they may be venerated still. The Bible has no record of how Isaiah died but the Jewish Talmud states he was sawn in half. Early Christian traditions of a miraculous fig tree, John the Baptist hiding in a wall with Holy Innocents, the places where Jesus's laundry was done, enrich the story of the Nativity and the Flight into Egypt. Martoni's delicious critique of the origin of balsam plants replaces one pretty tale with another. In a pre-truth world of miracle, myth and hearsay it is hard to draw the line between fact and fiction, if indeed Martoni would acknowledge the existence of a line.

Martoni understands and interprets his world in terms of the divine. God plays an active part in events and the lives of individuals. When he is rescued from drowning by a Saracen, who gets the credit? God, who sent the Saracen. God directly intervenes through miracles. Today the miraculous is usually regarded as 'supernatural', bending or breaking the laws of nature. For Martoni the miraculous is part of nature. Divine intervention is as natural as the weather. Miracles are marvellous not because they are unnatural but because they demonstrate God's benevolence.

Relics are a direct link between the material and the divine. They are physical proof of the existence of saints and the reality of the divine. The most precious are artefacts connected with Christ, the most potent being the Holy Cross. Relics derive miraculous power from their direct association with holy men and women. They are conduits from the material world to the other world where Christ and his mother and all human souls ultimately reside. Icons are similar conduits. Some icons acquire miraculous power or have miraculous origins but their primary function is to bear witness to the integration of the material and the divine and provide a channel to communicate between them. Relics also include buildings, plants and landscape. The Holy Sepulchre, miraculous trees, the seas and mountains of the Holy Land, are relics that surround us. By walking through them or among them the pilgrim takes part in the story and bears witness to its truth.

Is this way of looking at the world uniquely medieval? In a recent and excellent book on life in

Medieval England the author states that 'The word which best sums up the medieval attitude to the Devil, miracles and everything in between is superstition.' From a rational, secular, modern point of view this is arguable but not uniquely medieval. Famous pictures and statues still draw crowds of worshippers. Apologists might tell you that when we reverence a famous icon or give a gift to a statue, its power is not in the artefact, but helps us pray to whom it represents. In that case photocopies or plastic souvenirs from the gift shop would be as potent, which they patently are not, or there would be no homage and offerings to the original.

I have had my throat blessed by a candle on the feast of Saint Blaise. I have queued up to kiss relics of the true cross in Solihull and Dulwich. In Westminster in 2013 roses and candles were sold to people queueing through the night to venerate the relics of Saint Teresa of Lisieux, worshippers who included familiar faces from public life. On Mount Athos I have venerated the girdle of the Virgin that Martoni venerated. When it went on tour to Moscow there were queues a kilometre long to do the same, led by President Putin. You may venerate several relics that Martoni describes, the head of Saint Macarius of Jerusalem for example, in Pittsburgh's Saint Antony's chapel, that boasts over five thousand relics acquired in Europe in the late nineteenth century. I have met an American lawyer who attributed his miraculous recovery from serious spinal debility to the intervention of Cardinal John Henry Newman, a miracle which is part of the case for the Cardinal's canonisation. As I write this, a million pilgrims from as far away as China and Venezuela and East Timor are expected in Fatima for the canonisation by Pope

Francis of two children to whom the Virgin Mary appeared in 1917. It follows papal confirmation of a miracle attributed to their intercession.

Martoni's world view may be unfashionable and derided by non-believers, but it belongs in the twenty-first century as well as the fourteenth.

JOHN MOLE

ACKNOWLEDGEMENTS

My wife Nuala has listened patiently in unsocial hours to my going on about our friend Nicola and made many useful comments and suggestions.

The Latin text of his journal is from the Revue de l'Orient Latin vol III Paris pub: Ernest Leroux 1895 pp 566-669.

The Latin text is included *Martoni's Pilgrimage - in English and Latin* ISBN: 978-0-9557569-9-3

The same volume of the Revue de l'Orient Latin pp 163-302, also contains Jacopo da Verona's pilgrimage guide 'Liber Peregrinationis'. It includes the sketch of Sinai used on the cover.

The French translation in Vers Jerusalem, ed. Michel Tarayre Paris pub Les Belles Lettres 2009 has helpful notes.

The St Catherine badge was made of lead in France. The picture is from the British Museum.

Corrections and comments would be gratefully received through my website *www.johnmole.com*

JOHN MOLE

John Mole was born in Birmingham, England. He lives in London and Greece. He has travelled extensively through Greece, Turkey and the Middle East for business and pleasure.

His love of travel around the Aegean has resulted in several books. The best-selling travel memoir *It's All Greek To Me!* is about life in a village on Evia / Euboea. The same place is the location of *The Hero of Negropont,* a novel about English Tourists exploring Ottoman Greece. *The Sultan's Organ* is a modern English version of the wonderful diary of an Elizabethan musician taking a self-playing organ and clock through the Mediterranean to Constantinople.

These and his other books are on Amazon and Kindle and in selected bookshops.

www.johnmole.com

JOHN MOLE

THE SULTAN'S ORGAN

The diary of Thomas Dallam 1599
put into modern English by
John Mole

In 1598 merchants of the City of London paid for a Present to be given by Queen Elizabeth to Sultan Mehmet III of Turkey. In return they hoped to secure trading concessions and to turn the Sultan's military might on England's Spanish enemies. The Present was a carved, painted and gilded cabinet about sixteen feet high, six feet wide and five feet deep. It contained a chiming clock with jewel-encrusted moving figures combined with an automatic organ, which could play tunes on its own for six hours.

With it went Thomas Dallam, musician and organ builder. He encountered storms, volcanoes, exotic animals, foreign food, good wine, pirates, brigands, Moors, Turks, Greeks, Jews, beautiful women, barbarous men, kings and pashas, armies on the march, janissaries, eunuchs, slaves, dwarves and finally the most powerful man in the known world, the Great Turk himself.

Dallam was the first foreigner to record a glimpse into the Sultan's harem and the first to cross mainland Greece. His diary is a wonderful traveler's tale that will richly entertain and inform travellers to Greece and Turkey and fans of Elizabethan history.

Published by Fortune Books
www.fortunebooks.org
ISBN: 9 780955 756924

IT'S ALL GREEK TO ME!

Sun, Sheep and Sea, Ruins, Retsina – and Real Greeks.
A love affair with Greece.

A little whitewashed house with a blue door and blue shutters on an unspoiled island in a picturesque village next to the beach with a taverna round the corner - in your dreams Moley. Welcome to a tumbledown ruin on a hillside with no road, no water, no electricity, no roof, no floor, no doors, no windows and twenty years of goat dung.

Come to our village on Evia. Meet Elpida, who cures bad backs with a raw egg and spells; Ajax the death-dealing butcher; Saint John the goat-headed saint; beautiful Eleni yearning for Düsseldorf; old man Christos, dug up on a sunny summer morning; sun-touched Dionysos dancing like an English tourist; the family saved from a watery grave and Hector their dog, a mutant specially bred to frighten little children.

Here is timeless, rural Greece - catch it before it goes.

Published by Nicholas Brealey (including Kindle)
www.fortunebooks.org
ISBN: 9 781857 883756

THE HERO OF NEGROPONT

A travel book, a comedy, a history, a fiction.

To escape debt and summonses, rakish Lord Exford is exiled in 1788 to Constantinople with a prudish tutor and a truculent artist. They are shipwrecked on a Greek island ruled by a Turkish pasha and populated with stories of passion and delusion. Star-crossed lovers, renegades and minstrels, pirates and djinn are just some of the characters our travellers encounter. They also meet Amelia Burbage, a botanist, feminist and intrepid explorer, with her Syrian servant and an irascible camel. Befuddled by love, hashish and his classical education, Exford's tutor takes on the might of the Sultan and it is left to the wily Exford to deliver his eccentric band from an unspeakable fate.

Between Ancient Greece and Modern Greece were four centuries of Ottoman Greece. Join Lord Exford on his grand tour.

Published by Fortune Books
www.fortunebooks.org
ISBN: 9 780955 756931